Glorious Soups and Breads

by Nancy Brannon

Illustrated by Debbie Hummel

ConAmore
Publishing

Also by the author:

Feasting in the Forest
(co-authored with husband, Dave Brannon)
ISBN 0-9623036-0-7

and

The Lighter Side of Italy
ISBN 0-9623036-2-3

First Edition 1994

ISBN 0-9623036-4-X

Library of congress Catalogue Number 94-094231

Published by ConAmore Publishing, Box 7, Cody, WY 82414

Original Illustrations by Debbie Hummel

Lithography by R.W. Patterson Printing, Benton Harbor, MI 49022

♥

For my Dad...who convinced me that I could accomplish
anything I set out to do...and who made
the best pot of Bouillabaisse I ever tasted!

♥

Introduction

    For years I have said that I could LIVE on good homemade soups and breads. I hope that after reading thru this collection of recipes, you'll feel the same way. The really nice thing about "homemade", is that you know it's fresh and natural...no preservatives, no chemicals...nothing but the pure fresh ingredients you've added yourself.

    Soups are so easy! And, while most require a little time to simmer before they reach the peak of flavor, the actual amount of time you'll spend on each recipe is minimal and <u>worth it</u>...particularly considering the rave reviews you'll get from family and guests. While you CAN use canned broths (or stock made from bouillon cubes), I've included recipes for healthy homemade stocks, if you want to go that extra mile.

    Breads can be a little intimidating if you're not used to working with yeast. But if you follow these easy, step-by-step instructions, you'll turn out fabulous loaves and rolls every time...guaranteed! (Look for the helpful tips scattered throughout the chapter on breads.) Try it! You'll wonder why you don't bake bread more often. The recipes are delicious...and as an added bonus, the aromas in your kitchen will drive your family (and neighbors!) crazy!

Nancy

Table of Contents

Soups

Rich and Creamy

Preparation time: 30 minutes   **Cooking Time:** 20 minutes

Shrimp Bisque

2 tablespoons Butter
1 cup chopped Onion
1 cup shredded Carrot
1 cup sliced Celery
2 tablespoons Flour
1 tablespoon Tomato Paste
4 cups Chicken Broth
1 pound cooked, peeled and deveined
"Salad-style" Shrimp
1 cup Whipping Cream
2 tablespoons fresh Lemon Juice
2 tablespoons Cream Sherry
1/8 teaspoon ground Nutmeg
1/8 teaspoon ground White Pepper
Salt to taste
Chopped fresh Cilantro to garnish

In a medium stock pot, sauté the onion, carrot and celery in the butter until translucent...about 5 minutes. Stir in the flour, then the tomato paste. Gradually add the chicken broth and then bring the soup to a boil. Add the shrimp and simmer for 15 minutes. Put the soup in a blender and puree it until very smooth. Return the soup to the pan and add the cream, lemon juice, sherry, nutmeg and white pepper. Bring the soup to a simmer...taste and add salt as desired. Serve hot, garnished with a little chopped fresh cilantro. Makes 2½ quarts.

Serving Size: 6 ounces   **Calories:** 209   **Total Fat:** 13.6 grams (59%)
Sat. Fat: 8.0 grams   **Cholesterol:** 141 mgs.
Sodium: 643 mgs.   **Carbohydrates:** 6.7 grams

Preparation time: 30 minutes   **Cooking Time:** 45 minutes

Cheddar Chowder

2 tablespoons Butter
1 cup coarsely chopped Onion
1 cup sliced Celery
½ cup shredded Carrot
½ cup finely diced Sweet Red Bell Pepper
½ cup finely diced Green Bell Pepper
1 20-ounce package frozen Corn
2 cups (about 1½ pounds) peeled and
diced Russet Potatoes
4 cups Chicken Broth
1 12-ounce bottle Dark Beer
¼ teaspoon ground Cayenne Pepper
2 cups Half-and-Half
6 ounces grated Sharp Cheddar Cheese
Salt to taste

In a large stock pot over medium heat, sauté the onion and celery until transparent. Add all but the last three remaining ingredients. Bring to a boil over medium-high heat. Reduce the heat and simmer for 30 minutes, or until the potatoes are tender. Add the half and half and cheddar stirring constantly, until the soup resumes a gentle boil. Taste and season with salt, if desired. Serve hot. Makes 2½ quarts.

Serving Size: 8 ounces   **Calories:** 240   **Total Fat:** 12.7 grams (45%)
Sat. Fat: 8 grams   **Cholesterol:** 39 mgs.
Sodium: 257 mgs.   **Carbohydrates:** 24 grams

Belgian Waterzooi

An "American-ized" version of the famous lemon-chicken soup.

2 tablespoons Butter
2 cups sliced Leeks (white portion only)
1 cup chopped Onion
2 cups sliced Celery
12 cups Chicken Broth
1 cup peeled and sliced Carrots
½ teaspoon coarsely ground Black Pepper
1 small peeled whole Onion, studded with 6 whole Cloves
2 tablespoons chopped fresh Parsley
1 teaspoon dried Thyme
1 Bay Leaf
½ teaspoon Salt
1 whole Chicken (about 4 pounds), quartered

❖

2 tablespoons Butter
2 tablespoons Flour
1 cup Dry White Wine
3 Egg Yolks
1 cup Heavy Cream
1 Lemon, cut into thin slices

In a large stock pot over medium-high heat, sauté the leeks, onion and celery in the butter until limp. Add the chicken broth, carrots, pepper, whole onion studded with cloves, parsley, thyme, bay leaf, salt and chicken. Bring to a boil, then reduce the heat and simmer (uncovered) for 1 hour, or until the chicken is very tender. Remove the chicken from the soup. Place it on a platter until it is cool to the touch. Remove and discard the skin, fat and bones. Cut the meat into large chunks and return it to the soup. In a small saucepan over low heat, melt the butter... then, stir in the flour, blending well. Gradually add 2 or 3 ladles of the hot soup, whisking with a wire whip. When well combined and free of lumps, pour the mixture into the soup, stirring well. Add the wine, and bring the soup back to a simmer. In a small bowl, whisk together the egg yolks and the cream. Remove the soup from the heat. Pour the egg yolk mixture into the soup, stirring constantly. Serve hot, garnished with a slice of lemon.

Makes 5 quarts.

Serving Size: 8 ounces   Calories: 242   Total Fat: 17 grams (64%)
Sat. Fat: 6.9 grams   Cholesterol: 90 mgs.
Sodium: 599 mgs.   Carbohydrates: 5.13 grams

Preparation time: 15 minutes   **Cooking Time:** 45 minutes

Cream of Celeriac Soup

4 cups peeled and shredded Celeriac (Celery Root)
(about 1½ to 2 pounds)
2 cups sliced Leeks (white portion only)
6 cups Chicken Broth
1/8 teaspoon ground White Pepper
½ teaspoon Salt
¼ teaspoon Nutmeg
2 cups Half-and-Half
Chopped fresh Parsley for garnish

Place the shredded celeriac, sliced leeks (rinsed thoroughly), chicken broth, pepper, salt and nutmeg in a large stock pot over medium-high heat. Bring to a boil, then reduce the heat to a simmer and cook, uncovered, for 30 minutes, or until vegetables are very tender. Remove the vegetables from the broth, reserving both. Pureé the vegetables in a blender or food processor until very smooth. Return to stock pot with broth. Stir well. Add the half-and-half and heat through. Serve hot, garnished with chopped parsley. Makes 3+ quarts.

Serving Size: 8 ounces   **Calories:** 94.3   **Total Fat:** 5 grams (47%)
Sat. Fat: 2.8 grams   **Cholesterol:** 13.7 mgs.
Sodium: 502 mgs.   **Carbohydrates:** 8.5 grams

Preparation time: 20 minutes   **Cooking Time:** 45 minutes

New England Clam Chowder

6 slices of Bacon, cut into ¼" strips
1 cup coarsely chopped Onion
1 cup thinly sliced Celery
1/2 cup peeled and finely diced Carrots
3 cups peeled and diced Russet Potatoes
6 cups Chicken Broth
½ cup chopped fresh Parsley
4 10-ounce cans Baby Clams (with juice)
2 8-ounce bottles Clam Juice
¼ teaspoon ground White Pepper
1 quart Half-and-Half
Enough Gold Medal Wondra® to thicken as
desired (about ¼ cup)
2 tablespoons fresh Lemon Juice
Salt to taste

In a large stock pot over medium heat, sauté the bacon until crisp. Drain, reserving bacon bits and 1 tablespoon of the fat. Discard the remaining fat. Add the onion to the bacon bits and continue sautéing until the onions are limp. Add the celery, carrots, potatoes, chicken broth, parsley, baby clams (with juice), clam juice, and white pepper. Bring to a boil. Reduce the heat and simmer for 30 minutes, or until potatoes are tender. Add the half-and-half and return to a simmer. Gradually sprinkle the Wondra® over the top of the soup, stirring constantly, until the desired thickness is reached. (Wait a few minutes between additions, so that the flour has a chance to cook, before you decide whether to add more.) Stir in the lemon juice...then taste and add salt, if desired. Makes 5 quarts.

Serving Size: 8 ounces   **Calories:** 212   **Total Fat:** 8 grams (35%)
Sat. Fat: 4 grams   **Cholesterol:** 58 mgs.
Sodium: 459 mgs.   **Carbohydrates:** 15 grams

Preparation time: 45 minutes   **Cooking Time:** 1 hour

Cream of Asparagus Soup

2 pounds fresh Asparagus
2 tablespoons Butter
½ cup chopped Onion
¼ cup chopped Celery
1 tablespoon chopped Shallots
1 cup peeled and diced Potato
8 cups Chicken Broth
¼ teaspoon ground White Pepper
½ cup Heavy Whipping Cream
¼ cup Sour Cream
Salt to taste

❖

2 hard boiled Eggs, grated, for garnish

Remove just the tips from the asparagus (reserving the stalks) and blanch them in boiling water for 1 minute. Drain and plunge into ice water to stop the cooking. Drain again, and set aside. Cut the asparagus stalks into 1" pieces, discarding only the very tough ends. Melt the butter in a large stock pot over medium heat. Add the asparagus stalks, onion, celery, and shallots and sauté for 5-7 minutes, or until limp. Add the potato, chicken broth, and pepper. Bring to a boil. Reduce heat and simmer (uncovered) for 45 minutes, or until vegetables are very tender. Meanwhile, combine the whipping cream and sour cream in a small bowl. Set aside. Purée the soup in batches in a blender. Return it to the pot, and bring back up to steaming. Do not boil. Stir in the mixed creams. Taste and add salt as desired. To serve, ladle into bowls, and garnish with a few asparagus tips and a little grated hard boiled egg. Makes 3½ quarts.

Serving Size: 8 ounces   **Calories:** 113   **Total Fat:** 7.4 grams (57%)
Sat. Fat: 4.0 grams   **Cholesterol:** 48.2 mgs.
Sodium: 516 mgs.   **Carbohydrates:** 7.6 grams

Domatòsoupa

Greek Tomato Soup

4 14½-ounce cans peeled and diced Tomatoes (with juice)
2 cups Chicken Broth
1 teaspoon dried Oregano Leaves
1 teaspoon dried Basil
1 teaspoon dried Thyme
¼ teaspoon freshly ground Black Pepper
2 tablespoons Butter

❖

3 tablespoons Butter
3 tablespoons Flour
2 cups Whole Milk
Salt to taste
Chopped fresh Parsley to garnish

Combine all of the ingredients down to the ❖ in a large stock pot over medium heat. Bring the soup to a boil, and then reduce the heat and simmer the soup, uncovered, for 20-30 minutes, or until mixture has thickened. Pureé the soup in a blender or food processor for 1-2 minutes, or until very smooth, and return it to the stock pot. In a small saucepan, melt the butter, then stir in the flour and cook until bubbly. Gradually incorporate the milk, stirring constantly. Cook over low to medium heat until the sauce thickens. Then, whisk the sauce into the soup. Heat to a slow boil, then taste and add salt as desired. Remove from the heat and serve, garnished with the parsley. Makes 3 quarts.

Serving Size: 8 ounces   **Calories:** 110   **Total Fat:** 6.7 grams (53%)
Sat. Fat: 3.9 grams   **Cholesterol:** 18.5 mgs.
Sodium: 511 mgs.   **Carbohydrates:** 9.7 grams

Gingered Pumpkin Soup

2 tablespoons Butter
1 cup chopped Onion
4 cups Chicken Broth
2 tablespoons grated fresh Ginger
1 cup Orange Juice
½ cup Light Rum
1 29-ounce can cooked Pumpkin
1 cup Whipping Cream

❖

Snipped fresh Chives to garnish

In a Dutch oven over medium heat, sauté the onions in the butter until limp. Add the chicken broth, grated ginger, orange juice and rum. Bring to a boil. Reduce heat, cover and simmer slowly for 30 minutes. Stir in the pumpkin and whipping cream, and bring back to a boil, stirring frequently. Serve hot, garnished with snipped chives. Makes 2½ quarts.

Serving Size: 8 ounces   **Calories:** 214   **Total Fat:** 9.5 grams (39%)
Sat. Fat: 5.7 grams   **Cholesterol:** 29.7 mgs.
Sodium: 467 mgs.   **Carbohydrates:** 24.6 grams

New Orleans Cream of Corn Soup

2 tablespoons Butter
¾ cup chopped Onion
4 cups Chicken Broth
3 cups frozen or fresh Corn
¼ teaspoon ground White Pepper
1 teaspoon Tabasco©
2 cups Half and Half
Enough Gold Medal Wondra© to thicken (about 3 tablespoons)
Salt to taste

❖

½ Whipping Cream
Chopped fresh Parsley to garnish

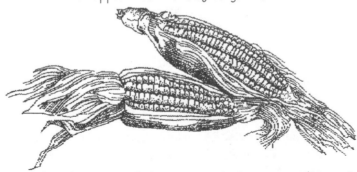

In a large stock pot over medium heat, sauté the onion in the butter until limp. Add the chicken broth, corn, pepper and Tabasco©. Bring to a boil. Reduce the heat and simmer (covered) for 15 minutes. Stir in the half and half and bring back to a simmer. Sprinkle the Wondra© over the top of the soup, stirring constantly, until the desired thickness is reached. Taste and add salt, if desired. Whip the whipping cream in a small bowl and top each serving with a dollop of cream and a sprinkling of parsley.
Makes 2 quarts.

Serving Size: 8 ounces   **Calories:** 122   **Total Fat:** 8.4 grams (62%)
Sat. Fat: 4.9 grams   **Cholesterol:** 26.3 mgs.
Sodium: 587 mgs.   **Carbohydrates:** 6.5 grams

Preparation time: 20 minutes   **Cooking Time:** 45 minutes

Creamy Barley Soup with Prosciutto

2 tablespoons Butter
2 tablespoons minced Shallots
8 cups Chicken Broth
1 cup Pearl Barley
½ teaspoon freshly ground Black Pepper
½ teaspoon Salt (or to taste)
1 teaspoon dried Thyme
¼ teaspoon ground Nutmeg
½ cup chopped fresh Parsley
1 10-ounce package frozen Peas
1 cup peeled and diced Carrots

❖

1 cup Heavy Cream
¼ pound thinly sliced Prosciutto (Italian Ham), cut into thin julienne strips
1 tablespoon of grated Parmesan Cheese per serving for garnish

Sauté the shallots in the butter in a large stock pot over medium-high heat until limp. Add the remaining ingredients (except the cream, ham and the Parmesan), in the order given. Bring to a boil. Reduce the heat and simmer, uncovered, for 45 minutes, or until the barley is very tender. Stir in the cream and bring the soup back to a simmer. Taste and add extra salt, if desired. Serve hot, garnished with a little of the Prosciutto and Parmesan. Makes 3+ quarts.

Serving Size: 8 ounces   **Calories:** 231   **Total Fat:** 12.8 grams (50%)
Sat. Fat: 8.0 grams   **Cholesterol:** 42.2 mgs.
Sodium: 904 mgs.   **Carbohydrates:** 18 grams

Preparation time: 20 minutes   **Cooking Time:** 30 minutes

Sour Cream Mushroom Soup

3 tablespoons Butter
1 cup chopped Onion
½ pound sliced fresh Mushrooms
1 teaspoon dried Tarragon
¼ cup Flour
5 cups Beef Broth
1 tablespoon Lemon Juice
¼ teaspoon freshly ground Black Pepper
1 cup Sour Cream
Salt to taste

❖

Chopped fresh Tarragon (if available), or chopped fresh Parsley to garnish

In a large stock pot over medium heat, sauté the onion until limp. Add the mushrooms and tarragon and continue to sauté until the mushrooms begin to lightly brown. Remove from heat, and sprinkle the flour over the mushrooms. Stir well. Gradually add the beef broth, and then the lemon juice and pepper. Bring to a boil. Then, reduce the heat and simmer (uncovered) for 30 minutes, stirring occasionally. Just before serving, stir in the sour cream. Serve hot, garnished with chopped fresh tarragon (or parsley). Makes 2 quarts

Serving Size: 8 ounces   **Calories:** 141   **Total Fat:** 10.9 grams (68%)
Sat. Fat: 6.6 grams   **Cholesterol:** 24.4 mgs.
Sodium: 684 mgs.   **Carbohydrates:** 7.7 grams

Dilly Cream of Leek Soup

2-2½ pounds Leeks (about 4-5 large)
2 tablespoons Butter
1 tablespoon dried Dill Weed
6 cups Chicken Broth
4 cups peeled and diced Russet Potatoes
¼ teaspoon freshly ground Black Pepper
2 cups Half and Half
Salt to taste

❖

1 tablespoon Sour Cream per serving for garnish
Fresh Dill Weed sprigs (or dried dill weed) for garnish

Trim the root ends from the leeks and remove any tough outer leaves. Slice the leeks into ¼" rounds and place them in a colander. Rinse them under cold, running water to remove any sand. In a large stock pot, melt the butter, and then sauté the leeks with the dill weed, until limp. Add the chicken broth, potatoes and pepper. Bring to a boil over medium heat.

Simmer for 40-45 minutes, or until the vegetables are very tender. Process the soup in batches in a blender (or food processor fitted with a steel blade) until smooth. Return the soup to the stock pot, and add the half and half. Bring the soup back up to a simmer. Taste and add salt as desired. To serve, ladle the soup in bowls and top with a dollop of sour cream and a sprig of dill. Makes 4+ quarts.

Serving Size: 8 ounces   Calories: 181   Total Fat: 8.4 grams (41%)
Sat. Fat: 5 grams   Cholesterol: 20.5 mgs.
Sodium: 386 mgs.   Carbohydrates: 22.4 grams

♥
Leeks
(Allium Porrum)

A member of the lily family, leeks originated in the Mediterranean. With a flavor similar to onion, but more delicate, it lends itself particularly well to soups. The whiteness of the bulb is due to "blanching"...piling dirt around the stalk to keep it from the sun. Because it doesn't have a "bulb" in the same sense as an onion, it tends to collect sand and dirt down in its leaves. So, be sure to slice it into rounds or slit the leek lengthwise and rinse it well, before adding it to the recipe.

Preparation time: 15 minutes   **Cooking Time:** 45 minutes

Shrimp and Sweet Corn Chowder

2 tablespoons Butter
1 cup chopped Onion
8 cups Chicken Broth
3 cups peeled and diced Russet Potatoes
1 teaspoon Salt
¼ teaspoon ground White Pepper
1 cup Whipping Cream
½ pound Large Green (raw) Shrimp, peeled and deveined
2 cups fresh Sweet Corn, cut from the cob
3 ounces grated Sharp Cheddar Cheese

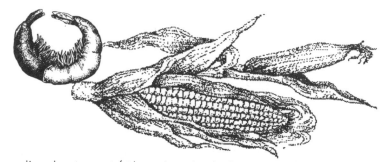

In a stock pot over medium heat, sauté the onions in the butter until limp. Add the chicken broth, potatoes, salt, white pepper, and whipping cream. Bring to a boil. Reduce the heat and simmer (uncovered) for 30 minutes. Add the shrimp and sweet corn. Return to a simmer, and cook for 10 minutes, or until the shrimp are firm, but tender. Remove the soup from the heat and stir in the cheese. Stir well. Serve immediately. Makes 3½ quarts.

Serving Size: 8 ounces   **Calories:** 185   **Total Fat:** 11.2 grams (54%)
Sat. Fat: 6.5 grams   **Cholesterol:** 65.7 mgs.
Sodium: 698 mgs.   **Carbohydrates:** 12.4 grams

Preparation time: 30 minutes   **Cooking Time:** 30 minutes

Zuppa di Cipolle Gratinata

A Creamy Italian Onion Soup Topped with Melted Cheese

1½ tablespoons Olive Oil
4 cups sliced Onion
½ teaspoon freshly ground Black Pepper
¼ cup All Purpose White Flour
6 cups Beef Broth
½ cup Dry White Wine
2 cups Half-and-Half
Salt to taste

❖

1 tablespoon Butter
4 slices stale Wheat Bread
½ teaspoon Garlic Salt
½ teaspoon dried Oregano Leaves

❖

½-ounce sliced Gruyere or Swiss Cheese per
serving for garnish (6 ounces, total)

In a large stock pot over medium heat, brown the onions in the olive oil until well caramelized (about 15-20 minutes) stirring frequently. Remove from heat and stir in the pepper and flour until well combined. Gradually add 1 cup of the beef broth, stirring to avoid lumps. Add the remaining broth, the wine and half-and-half and return the pot to the stove. Bring to a boil and let the soup thicken. Taste and add salt, if desired. Meanwhile, in a large skillet over medium heat, melt the butter and coat the entire bottom of the skillet. Cut the bread slices into quarters and fry them in the butter (seasoned with the garlic salt and oregano), tossing constantly, until nicely browned and crisp. Remove from heat and set aside.   Just before serving, preheat the broiler to high. Ladle the soup into oven-proof crocks. Top each bowl with a crouton and a slice of cheese. Broil just until the cheese is bubbly. Serve hot.

Makes 3 quarts.

Serving Size: 8 ounces   **Calories:** 203   **Total Fat:** 12.6 grams (55%)
Sat. Fat: 6.6 grams   **Cholesterol:** 33 mgs.
Sodium: 604 mgs.   **Carbohydrates:** 13 grams

Preparation time: 15 minutes   **Cooking Time:** 1 hour

Soúpa Avgolémono

Greek Egg and Lemon Soup

6 cups Chicken Broth
1 pound boneless-skinless Chicken Thighs
½ tablespoon dried Oregano Leaves
1 Bay Leaf
¼ teaspoon freshly ground Black Pepper
¾ cup uncooked Long Grain Rice
6 whole Large Eggs
½ cup fresh Lemon Juice
Salt to taste

In a large stock pot, combine the chicken broth, chicken thighs, oregano, bay leaf, and pepper. Bring to a boil over medium heat, then reduce the heat and simmer, covered, for 30 minutes. Add the rice and continue to simmer for 25 to 30 minutes, or until the rice is tender. Remove the chicken and bay leaf from the soup and set aside to cool. When cool enough to handle, shred the meat back into the soup. Just before serving, combine the eggs and lemon juice in a blender, blending well. With the blender running, add a ladle or two of the hot broth (no meat or rice), to raise the temperature. Next, add the egg and lemon mixture to the soup, stirring constantly. Heat thoroughly, but do not allow to boil, as this will curdle the soup. Serve hot. Makes 3 quarts.

Serving Size: 8 ounces   **Calories:** 182   **Total Fat:** 7.6 grams (39%)
Sat. Fat: 2.2 grams   **Cholesterol:** 153 mgs.
Sodium: 586 mgs.   **Carbohydrates:** 9.8 grams

Preparation time: 20-30 minutes   **Cooking Time:** 45 minutes

Purée of Leek Soup with Roquefort

A rich and elegant soup fit for a posh dinner party!
(Definitely *not* for those on a diet!)

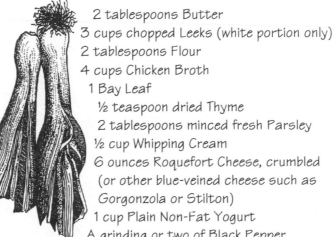

2 tablespoons Butter
3 cups chopped Leeks (white portion only)
2 tablespoons Flour
4 cups Chicken Broth
1 Bay Leaf
½ teaspoon dried Thyme
2 tablespoons minced fresh Parsley
½ cup Whipping Cream
6 ounces Roquefort Cheese, crumbled
(or other blue-veined cheese such as
Gorgonzola or Stilton)
1 cup Plain Non-Fat Yogurt
A grinding or two of Black Pepper

In a stock pot over medium heat, sauté the leeks in the butter until limp. Add the flour and stir well to coat the leeks. Gradually add the broth, then the bay leaf, thyme and parsley. Bring to a boil, then reduce the heat and simmer (covered) for 30-45 minutes, or until the leeks are very tender. Remove the bay leaf and discard. Purée the soup in a blender, and then return it to the pot. Add the cream, and return the soup to a boil. Remove the soup from the heat, and stir in the cheese, yogurt and pepper. Serve immediately. Makes 4 servings (1 quart).

Serving Size: 8 ounces   **Calories:** 390   **Total Fat:** 28.4 grams (64%)
Sat. Fat: 17.7 grams   **Cholesterol:** 88.2 mgs.
Sodium: 903 mgs.   **Carbohydrates:** 20.7 grams

Hot and Spicy

Preparation time: 1½ hours   **Cooking Time:** Up to 5 hours

Mexican Three-Bean Chili

½ cup Dry Red Beans
½ cup Dry Black (Turtle) Beans
½ cup Dry Navy (Pea) Beans
1-1½ pounds Chorizo or other Mexican sausage
1 cup chopped Onion
12 cups Beef Broth
2 14½-ounce cans diced Tomatoes (with juice)
1 4½-ounce can chopped Mild Green Chilis
¼ cup chopped Green Bell Pepper
¼ cup chopped Sweet Red Bell Pepper
1½ tablespoons Chili Powder
2 tablespoons Worcestershire Sauce
2 teaspoons Cumin Seed
1 tablespoon dried Oregano
¼ cup chopped fresh Cilantro
2 teaspoons Salt
½ teaspoon freshly ground Black Pepper

Combine the three types of beans in a large bowl and cover with boiling water. Let stand for 1 hour.
Meanwhile, remove the casing from the sausage and brown it in a large skillet, breaking it up with a
spoon (meat should be chunky). Drain as much fat from the cooked meat as you can. Add the onion
and sauté until transparent. Place the meat mixture in a large stock pot over medium-high heat. Add
the remaining ingredients in the order given, drainiing and adding the beans as soon as they are ready.
Bring to a boil. Reduce the heat and simmer for 4-5 hours, or until the beans are tender.

Makes 5 quarts.

Serving Size: 8 ounces   **Calories:** 154   **Total Fat:** 9.4 grams (55%)
Sat. Fat: 3.3 grams   **Cholesterol:** 26.6 mgs.
Sodium: 1152 mgs.   **Carbohydrates:** 7.2 grams

Preparation time: 40 minutes   **Cooking Time:** 1½ hours

Pozole

Southwestern Hominy Stew

8 cups Chicken Broth
1 Turkey Thigh/Drumstick (about 1½-2 pounds)
1 large, meaty Smoked Ham Hock (about 1-1½ pounds)
1 tablespoon dried Oregano Leaves
1 teaspoon Cumin Seeds, crushed
1½ cups chopped Onion
1 cup chopped Celery
½ teaspoon freshly ground Black Pepper
1 4-ounce can chopped Mild Green Chilies
1 cup Medium Hot Salsa
2 14½-ounce cans Golden Hominy (with juice)
Salt to taste

❖

6-8 Corn Tortillas (6"-7" diameter)
4 cups Vegetable Oil for deep frying

❖

2 teaspoons Green Chili Salsa per serving for garnish
1 tablespoon grated Cheddar Cheese per serving for garnish

In a very large stock pot over medium-high heat, combine the chicken broth, turkey, ham shank, oregano, cumin seeds, onion, pepper, green chilies, salsa and hominy. Bring to a boil, then reduce the heat and simmer (uncovered) for 1-1½ hours, or until the meat is very tender. With a slotted spoon, remove the meats from the broth and shred the meat back into the soup...discarding the bones and skin. Taste the soup and add salt as desired. Meanwhile, in a large, deep skillet, bring the vegetable oil up to 375° using a meat thermometer to test the temperature. Stack the tortillas, and with a sharp knife, cut them into ¼" wide strips. Fry the tortilla strips a handful at a time until crisp and lightly brown (about 1 minute). Drain on paper towels and reserve. When the soup is done, ladle it into bowls and top with green chili salsa, tortilla strips and cheddar cheese. Makes 5 quarts.

Serving Size: 8 ounces + toppings   **Calories:** 312   **Total Fat:** 17 grams (50%)
Sat. Fat: 6.1 grams   **Cholesterol:** 74.6 mgs.
Sodium: 739 mgs.   **Carbohydrates:** 14.2 grams

Preparation time: 30 minutes   **Cooking Time:** 1 hour 15 minutes

Cajun Gumbo

2 tablespoons Butter
1 tablespoon Olive Oil
1 cup chopped Onion
2 teaspoons minced Garlic
1 cup chopped Green Bell Pepper
8 cups Chicken Broth
1½ pounds boneless-skinless Chicken Thighs
1 cup diced Ham
¼ cup chopped fresh Parsley
2 14½-ounce cans diced Tomatoes
1 teaspoon dried Thyme
1 tablespoon Gumbo File Powder
½ teaspoon Tabasco® Sauce
1 10-ounce package frozen Okra, defrosted and sliced
2 cups shucked Oysters
1 pound small, peeled Green (raw) Shrimp
Salt and freshly ground Black Pepper to taste
5 cups cooked Rice

In a large stock pot, heat the butter and olive oil over medium heat, and sauté the onion, garlic and bell pepper until limp. Add the chicken broth, chicken thighs, ham, parsley, tomatoes, thyme, file powder, and Tabasco®, and bring to a boil. Reduce the heat and simmer for 1 hour, or until the.chicken is very tender. Remove the chicken from the broth and shred the meat back into the gumbo. Bring the soup back up to a simmer and add the okra, oysters and shrimp. Simmer over low heat for 15 minutes. Taste and add salt and pepper as desired. Serve hot over cooked rice. Makes 5+ quarts.

Serving Size: 8 ounces + ½ cup Rice   **Calories:** 311   **Total Fat:** 7.5 grams (22%)
Sat. Fat: 2.3 grams   **Cholesterol:** 99.3 mgs.
Sodium: 644 mgs.   **Carbohydrates:** 35.3 grams

Chile Blanco

"White" Chili with Chicken

1 pound dry White Northern Beans
8 cups boiling Water
2 tablespoons Olive Oil
¾ cup chopped Onion
2 teaspoons minced Garlic
12 cups Chicken Broth
2 4½-ounce cans Chopped Mild Green Chiles
1 tablespoon dried Oregano Leaves
2 tablespoons chopped fresh Cilantro
2 teaspoons ground Cumin
1 tablespoon minced Jalapeño Pepper
½ teaspoon freshly ground White Pepper
4 cups cooked, diced Chicken Breast (about 1½ pounds)
1 teaspoon salt, or to taste

❖

For garnishing (per serving):
6 ounces shredded Monterey Jack Cheese
¾ cup Mild Green Chili Salsa

Place the dry beans in a large bowl and pour in the boiling water. Let stand for 1 hour, and then drain and set aside. Meanwhile, in a large stock pot over medium heat, sauté the onion and garlic in the olive oil, until limp. Add the remaining ingredients (except the chicken, salt and garnishes) in the order given. Add the soaked beans, and bring the soup to a boil. Reduce the heat and simmer (uncovered) for 3 hours, or until the beans are tender. Add the chicken and salt. Stir well. Bring back to a simmer for 15 minutes longer. Taste and add extra salt if desired. To serve, ladle soup into bowls and top with 1 tablespoon (each) of cheese and salsa. Makes 4+ quarts.

Serving Size: 8 ounces   Calories: 214   Total Fat: 6.5 grams (27%)
Sat. Fat: 2.5 grams   Cholesterol: 35.6 mgs.
Sodium: 871 mgs.   Carbohydrates: 17.6 grams

Caribbean Crab and Spinach Soup

3 tablespoons Butter
1 cup chopped Onion
1 tablespoon minced Garlic
2 10-ounce packages frozen Chopped Spinach
5 cups Chicken Broth
1 13½-ounce can unsweetened Coconut Milk
1 teaspoon Salt
½ teaspoon coarse ground Black Pepper
2 teaspoons Tabasco®
½ pound Dungeness Crab Meat

In a large stock pot over medium heat, sauté the onion and garlic in the butter until limp. Add the remaining ingredients (except the crab meat) in the order given. Reduce the heat and simmer (uncovered), for 30 minutes.   Add the crab meat and simmer for 5 minutes longer.
Serve hot. Makes 2½ quarts.

Serving Size: 8 ounces   **Calories:** 154   **Total Fat:** 11.7 grams (65%)
Sat. Fat: 8.8 grams   **Cholesterol:** 29.1 mgs.
Sodium: 685 mgs.   **Carbohydrates:** 5.1 grams

New Orleans Frappéed Tomato Soup

1 cup Coffee Cream
3 cups Tomato Juice
½ cup grated Onion
½ cup grated Celery
½ teaspoon Tabasco® Sauce
¼ teaspoon Salt
1 teaspoon Worcestershire Sauce
1 cup crushed Ice

❖

6 large Celery Stalks, with leaves for garnish

Combine all the ingredients except the celery stalks in a blender. Blend well. Serve
in large stem glasses, garnished with a celery stalk. Pass the Tabasco® Sauce
for those who like a little extra zing!   Makes 6 servings (1½ quarts).

Serving Size: 8 ounces   **Calories:** 112   **Total Fat:** 7.9 grams (59%)
Sat. Fat: 4.8 grams   **Cholesterol:** 26.3 mgs.
Sodium: 602 mgs.   **Carbohydrates:** 9.8 grams

Preparation time: 30-40 minutes   Cooking Time: 1 hour

Caldo de Pollo

Spicy Mexican Chicken Soup

1 large, whole Chicken Breast
(about 1 pound)
(with bones and skin)
8 cups Chicken Broth
1 tablespoon Olive Oil
1 cup chopped Onion
3 teaspoons minced Garlic
½ cup chopped Celery
1 cup peeled and sliced Carrots
1½ cups sliced Zucchini
2 ears of fresh Sweet Corn, cut into 1" rounds
1 15½ -ounce can Garbanzo Beans (with juice)
1 4½-ounce can chopped Green Chiles
1 tablespoon chopped fresh Jalapeño Pepper
¼ cup chopped fresh Cilantro
2 tablespoons chopped fresh Oregano
(or 1 tablespoon dried Oregano Leaves)
¾ cup uncooked Long Grain Rice
(long cooking type)
½ teaspoon Salt
½ teaspoon freshly ground Black Pepper

❖

1 whole, ripe Avocado, peeled, pitted and diced
1 cup chunky Medium Salsa (fresh if available)
½ cup EACH shredded Monterey Jack Cheese and
Sharp Cheddar Cheese, mixed

In a large stock pot over medium-high heat, bring the chicken breast and broth to a boil. Reduce the heat, and simmer (uncovered) for 30 minutes. Meanwhile, in a large skillet, sauté the onion, garlic and celery in the olive oil until limp. Stage this mixture in a large bowl along with the next 11 ingredients (down to the ❖). Remove the chicken breast with a slotted spoon and let cool for 5-10 minutes, or until cool enough to handle. Strain and reserve the broth. Once cooled, remove the skin and bones from the breast and shred the meat. Set aside.   Bring the broth to a boil over medium heat. Add the vegetables. Reduce the heat and simmer (uncovered) for 30 minutes, or until rice is cooked. Taste, and add extra salt, if desired. To serve, place some shredded chicken, diced avocado, salsa and cheese in each bowl. Ladle the hot soup over the top. Serve immediately. Makes 4½ quarts.

Serving Size: 8 ounces   Calories: 193   Total Fat: 7.4 grams (34%)
Sat. Fat: 2.4 grams   Cholesterol: 25 mgs.
Sodium: 675 mgs.   Carbohydrates: 18.4 grams

♥

Buying Fresh Herbs
Fresh herbs, when you can find them (or grow them!) are always preferable to dried... although drying techniques today produce very acceptable results, if used within one year of purchase. Look for bright green colors and fragrant scents when buying fresh herbs.

Storage of Fresh Herbs
If you know that you will use them within a day or two...a sealed plastic bag in the refrigerator will do nicely. If you think it might be longer before you get to them, store them in a sealed glass jar, stems down, with about 1" of water in the refrigerator.

Southwestern Chunky Chili

2 pounds Beef Stew Meat, trimmed and cut into 1" dice
2 tablespoons Olive Oil
1 cup chopped Onion
1 cup thinly sliced Celery
½ cup diced Green Bell Pepper
½ cup diced Sweet Red Bell Pepper
1 14½-ounce can Golden Hominy (with juice)
1 14½-ounce can diced Tomatoes (with juice)
1 15½-ounce can small Red Beans (with juice)
1 8-ounce can Tomato Sauce
1 4½-ounce can chopped Mild Green Chilies
¼ teaspoon ground Cumin
2 teaspoons dried Oregano
¼ cup chopped fresh Parsley
2 teaspoons minced Garlic
6 cups Beef Broth
½ teaspoon freshly ground Black Pepper
2 tablespoons Tequila
Salt to taste

In a large stock pot over medium-high heat, warm the olive oil, and brown the meat quickly on all sides. Next, add the onion, celery and green and red bell peppers; sauté until the vegetables are limp. Then add all but the last two the remaining ingredients in the order given. Bring to a boil, then reduce the heat and simmer (partially covered) for 2 hours, or until meat is very tender. Just before serving, add the tequila and simmer 5 minutes. Then taste and add salt as desired. Makes 4½ quarts.

Serving Size: 8 ounces   **Calories:** 195   **Total Fat:** 7.8 grams (36%)
Sat. Fat: 2.5 grams   **Cholesterol:** 51.1 mgs.
Sodium: 804 mgs.   **Carbohydrates:** 11 grams

Chilled Sichuan Carrot Soup

1 tablespoon Olive Oil
1 cup chopped Onion
½ cup chopped Celery
2 teaspoons minced Garlic
¼ teaspoon Red Pepper Flakes
4 cups Chicken Broth
3 cups peeled and shredded Carrots
1 tablespoon grated fresh Ginger Root
¼ cup fresh Lime Juice
2 tablespoons Soy Sauce
2 tablespoons Smooth Peanut Butter
2 teaspoons Sugar
1 teaspoon Sesame Oil
¼ teaspoon ground Sichuan Peppercorns (optional)
1 cup Whole Milk

❖

Finely chopped Green Onions (tops only) for garnish

In a large stock pot over medium heat, sauté the onion, celery, garlic and red pepper flakes in the olive oil until the onions and celery are limp. Add the chicken broth and bring to a boil. Next, add the shredded carrots, ginger root. Bring back to a boil, then reduce the heat and simmer (uncovered) for 30 minutes, or until the vegetables are tender. Purée the soup in batches in a blender. Return it to the stock pot, and stir in the lime juice, soy sauce, peanut butter, sugar, sesame oil, ground peppercorns and milk. Heat through, but do not boil. Cover and refrigerate for at least 1 hour (or over night). To serve, ladle into chilled bowls, and garnish with a little chopped green onion. Makes 2 quarts.

Serving Size: 8 ounces   **Calories:** 111   **Total Fat:** 5.8 grams (45%)
Sat. Fat: 1.5 grams   **Cholesterol:** 3.9 mgs.
Sodium: 659 mgs.   **Carbohydrates:** 10.7 grams

Pueblo Lamb Stew

¼ cup Flour
2 tablespoons Chili Powder
1 teaspoon Salt
1 teaspoon freshly ground Black Pepper
2 pounds Lamb Stew Meat, cut into 1½" cubes
2 tablespoons Olive Oil
2 large Onions, peeled and cut into wedges
1 cup coarsely chopped Celery
3 teaspoons minced Garlic
2 large Sweet Red Bell Pepper, cut into 1" pieces
1 large Green Bell Pepper, cut into 1" pieces
2 tablespoons chopped fresh Serrano or Jalapeño Pepper
2 cups fresh or frozen Corn Kernels
2 14½-ounce cans peeled and diced Tomatoes
2 tablespoons dry Juniper Berries, crushed
8 cups Beef Broth

❖

Chopped Green Onions (including tops), for garnish

Place the flour, chili powder, salt and pepper in a bag, mixing well. Add the lamb and shake to coat evenly. In a large stock pot over high heat, quickly brown the seasoned lamb in the olive oil. Then add the remaining ingredients (except the green onions), in the order given. Bring to a boil and then reduce the heat to simmer (uncovered) for 1½ to 2 hours, or until the lamb is very tender. Serve hot, garnished with a little chopped green onion. Makes 4 quarts.

Serving Size: 8 ounces   **Calories:** 190   **Total Fat:** 7.2 grams (34%)
Sat. Fat: 2.2 grams   **Cholesterol:** 61.2 mgs.
Sodium: 582 mgs.   **Carbohydrates:** 9.6 grams

Cajun Black Bean Soup

2 tablespoons Olive Oil
1 cup chopped Onion
1 cup chopped Celery
½ cup chopped Green Bell Pepper
2 teaspoons minced Garlic
8 cups Water and
6 Vegetarian Vegetable Bouillon Cubes
(2 1/8 ounces each)
OR 8 cups Vegetarian Vegetable
Stock (see page 77)
1 pound dry Black (Turtle) Beans
2 tablespoons Paprika
2 tablespoons Chili Powder
½ teaspoon Cayenne Pepper
½ teaspoon ground Cumin
1½ - 2 pound Smoked Ham Hock
Salt to taste

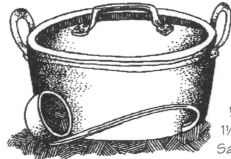

❖

To garnish:
1 cup Sour Cream
½ cup sliced Green Onions
3 Hard Boiled Eggs, chopped

In a large stock pot over medium heat, sauté the onion, celery, bell pepper and garlic in the olive oil until limp. Add the remaining ingredients (except the garnishes) in the order given. Bring to a boil, then reduce the heat and simmer (uncovered) for 3 hours (or until beans are tender), stirring occasionally. Remove the ham hock to a plate and let cool for 5-10 minutes, or until cool enough to handle. Remove the meat from the bone, and coarsely chop. Set aside. In a blender, or a food processor fitted with a steel blade, purée approximately half of the soup. Return it to the pot, and stir in the reserved meat. Bring the soup back up to a gentle simmer. Taste and add extra salt, if desired. Serve hot, garnished with about 1 tablespoon of sour cream, a little chopped green onion, and hard boiled egg.
Makes 4+ quarts.

Serving Size: 8 ounces   Calories: 325   Total Fat: 18.6 grams (51%)
Sat. Fat: 6.9 grams   Cholesterol: 95.7 mgs.
Sodium: 540 mgs.   Carbohydrates: 18.7 grams

Preparation time: 30 minutes   **Cooking Time:** 45 minutes

Tijuana Taco Soup

2 pounds Extra Lean Ground Beef
2 1¾-ounce packages Taco Seasoning Mix
1 cup chopped Onion
2 4½-ounce cans chopped Mild Green Chilies
1 15½-ounce can Small Red Beans (with juice)
1 15½-ounce can Great Northern Beans (with juice)
1 14½-ounce can Golden Hominy (with juice)
2 14½-ounce cans Whole Peeled Tomatoes (with juice)
4 cups Water

❖

1 tablespoon EACH Salsa, grated Sharp Cheddar Cheese,
and Sour Cream, per serving for garnish

In a large stock pot over medium-high heat, brown the ground beef with the taco seasoning mix, breaking it up into crumbles as it cooks. Add the onion, and continue cooking until the onion is limp. Then add the chilies, red beans, great northern beans, hominy, tomatoes, and water. Bring to a boil, then reduce the heat and simmer, uncovered, for 45 minutes. Taste and add extra salt if desired. To serve, ladle the soup into bowls and top each with salsa, cheese and sour cream. Taco chips make a great partner for this spicy soup! Makes nearly 5 quarts.

Serving Size: 8 ounces + toppings **Calories:** 260   **Total Fat:** 13.3 grams (46%)
Sat. Fat: 6.3 grams   **Cholesterol:** 58.7 mgs.
Sodium: 553 mgs.   **Carbohydrates:** 16.5 grams

Light and Healthy

Preparation time: 10 minutes   **Cooking Time:** 10 minutes

Japanese Egg Flower Soup

A lovely use for a little leftover chicken!

6 cups Chicken Broth
1½ tablespoons Soy Sauce
½ cup shredded fresh Spinach (well rinsed)
4 ounces shredded cooked Chicken (or Pork)
1 large Whole Egg, well beaten

Bring the chicken broth to a simmer over medium heat in a Dutch oven. Add the soy sauce, spinach and cooked chicken and return to a simmer. When the soup is simmering again, stir in the beaten egg. Serve at once. Makes 1½+ quarts.

Serving Size: 8 ounces   **Calories:** 73.6   **Total Fat:** 2.5 grams (32%)
Sat. Fat: .7 gram   **Cholesterol:** 44.1 mgs.
Sodium: 909 mgs.   **Carbohydrates:** 1.3 grams

Baked Potato Soup

4 strips of thick-sliced Bacon

3 tablespoons Flour

2 pounds Baked Russet Potatoes, with

skin (about 4 large potatoes) cooled and diced

1 cup chopped Onion

1 cup chopped Celery

¼ cup chopped fresh Parsley

4 cups Chicken Broth

1 tablespoon White Wine Vinegar

2 cups Half and Half Cream

Salt and Pepper to taste

½ cup chopped Green Onion Tops or Chives

Cut the bacon into ¼" strips and brown it evenly in a large stock pot over medium heat. Drain most of the bacon grease and discard, reserving 1 tablespoon. Return bacon grease to the stock pot and bring the temperature back up to medium. Then, add the onion and celery and sauté until limp. Toss the diced baked potatoes in the flour and then add them to the pot...browning lightly. Now add the parsley, chicken broth, vinegar and half and half. Bring to a boil, then reduce the heat and simmer, uncovered, for 30 minutes, stirring occasionally. Taste and season with salt and pepper as desired. Serve hot, topped with chopped green onion tops. Makes 2½ quarts.

Serving Size: 8 ounces   **Calories:** 176   **Total Fat:** 6.3 grams (32%)
Sat. Fat: 3.4 gr.   **Cholesterol:** 16.7 mgs.
Sodium: 414 mgs.   **Carbohydrates:** 24.5 grams.

* Note: While generally I am "anti-microwave" (I mean, you wouldn't really **cook** in one, would you???), they **are** wonderful for baking potatoes! They are fast, saving electricity...and they retain more of the moisture and nutrients than using a conventional oven. In this case, baking the potatoes in the microwave will take 8-10 minutes...while in a conventional oven, you'll need to allow 1-1½ hours.

Preparation time: 15 minutes   **Cooking Time:** 30 minutes

Minestra di Pomodoro e Basilico

Italian Tomato-Basil Soup

1 tablespoon Olive Oil
1 cup coarsely chopped Onion
2 teaspoons minced Garlic
2 14½-ounce cans Diced Tomatoes (with juice)
1½ cups fresh Basil Leaves, cut into thin strips
2 cups Beef Broth
1 teaspoon freshly ground Black Pepper
¼ cup Red Wine (preferably Chianti)
Salt to taste
1 tablespoon grated Parmesan per
serving to garnish

In a medium stock pot or Dutch oven, sauté the onion in the olive oil until transparent. Add the garlic, tomatoes, basil leaves, beef broth and pepper. Bring to a boil.   Add wine and return to a boil. Reduce the heat and simmer, uncovered for 30 minutes. Taste and season with salt as desired. Serve hot, garnished with Parmesan. Makes about 1½ quarts.

Serving Size: 8 ounces **Calories:** 90 **Total Fat:** 4 grams (38%)
Sat. Fat: 1.4 grams **Cholesterol:** 4 mgs.
Sodium: 682 mgs. **Carbohydrates:** 8.6 grams

Curried Apple Soup

6 cups Chicken Broth
3 cups peeled and chopped Apple
½ cup minced Onion
1½ cups Half and Half
½ teaspoon Salt
¼ teaspoon ground White Pepper
1 teaspoon Curry Powder
1 tablespoon Butter

❖

Wafer-thin Apple Slices to garnish

In a large Dutch oven, combine the chicken broth, apple and onion, and bring to a boil over medium heat.
Reduce the heat and simmer (covered) for about 30 minutes, or until the apples and onions are tender.
In batches, purée the soup in a blender (or food processor fitted with a steel blade) until smooth.
Return the soup to the pan and place on low heat. Stir in the remaining ingredients and heat through
(do not boil). To serve, ladle soup into bowls, and garnish with a few thin slices of apple.
Makes 2+ quarts.

Serving Size: 8 ounces   **Calories:** 109   **Total Fat:** 6.6 grams (54%)
Sat. Fat: 3.7 grams   **Cholesterol:** 17.4 mgs.
Sodium: 631 mgs.   **Carbohydrates:** 8.3 grams

Preparation Time: 30 minutes   **Cooking Time:** 1 hour

Minestra di Carciofi alla Fiorentine

Florentine Artichoke Soup

4 strips of Bacon, cut into ¼" pieces
1 cup coarsely chopped Onion
1 cup coarsely chopped Celery
8 cups Chicken Broth
1 10-ounce package frozen Chopped Spinach
15-ounce can Garbanzo Beans (with juice)
2 9-ounce packages frozen Artichoke Hearts
1 teaspoon freshly ground Black Pepper
2 pounds boneless-skinless Chicken Thighs
Salt to taste

In a large stock pot over medium heat, sauté the bacon until crisp. Drain and discard all but 1 tablespoon of the bacon grease. Add the onion and celery and continue sautéing until they are translucent. Then add the chicken broth, spinach, garbanzo beans, artichoke hearts and pepper. Bring to a boil and add the chicken. Return the soup to a boil, then reduce the heat to medium-low and simmer for 1 hour, or until the chicken is very tender. Lift the chicken from the soup and set it aside to cool for a few minutes. When cool enough to handle, shred the chicken and return it to the soup. Taste and season with additional salt, if desired.
Makes 4½ quarts.

Serving size: 8 ounces   **Calories:** 135   **Total Fat:** 3.8 grams (25%)
Sat. Fat: 1 gram . **Cholesterol:** 43 mgs.
Sodium: 575 mgs.   **Carbohydrates:** 10.3 grams

Preparation time: 15 minutes   **Cooking Time:** 45 minutes

Vegetable Soup Olé

Fast...Flavorful...and low in Fat!

1 tablespoon Olive Oil
1 cup coarsely chopped Onion
2 teaspoons minced Garlic
8 cups Chicken Broth
2 14½-ounce cans Diced Tomatoes (with juice)
1 16-ounce package frozen Cut Green Beans
1 16-ounce package frozen Sliced Carrots
1 16-ounce package frozen Corn
1 15½-ounce can Garbanzo Beans (with juice)
2 4½-ounce cans Chopped Mild Green Chilis
2 tablespoons fresh Lime Juice
1 tablespoon Chili Powder
½ teaspoon freshly ground Black Pepper
Salt to taste

❖

1 tablespoon grated Cheddar Cheese per serving to garnish

In a large stock pot, heat the oil, and sauté the onion until it just begins to brown. Add the garlic, chicken broth, tomatoes, green beans, carrots, corn, garbanzo beans, chilies, lime juice, chili powder and black pepper and bring to a boil. Reduce the heat and simmer, uncovered, for 45 minutes. Taste and add salt as desired. Serve hot, garnished with cheese.   Makes 5+ quarts.

Serving Size: 8 ounces   **Calories:** 100   **Total Fat:** 2 grams (16%)
Sat. Fat: Less than 1 gram   **Cholesterol:** 0 mgs.
Sodium: 624 mgs.   **Carbohydrates:** 17.5 grams

Chinese Shrimp and Snow Pea Soup

蝦荷蘭豆

4 cups Chicken Broth
¼ teaspoon Chinese Five-Spice Powder
1 tablespoon Soy Sauce
1 cup fresh Snow Pea Pods, stems removed
1 tablespoon sliced Green Onion
1 cup (about 6 ounces) peeled, deveined and
precooked Bay Shrimp

Bring the chicken broth to a boil over medium heat.
Add the Five-Spice powder and soy sauce...stirring well.
Add the snow pea pods and return to a boil.
Reduce heat to simmer. Add shrimp and simmer,
uncovered, for 5 minutes. Serve immediately,
garnished with green onion. Makes 1 quart.

Serving Size: 8 ounces   **Calories:** 72.4   **Total Fat:** 1.4 grams (18%)
Sat. Fat: Less than 1 gram   **Cholesterol:** 60.3 mgs.
Sodium: 822 mgs.   **Carbohydrates:** 3.1 grams

Preparation Time: 15 minutes   **Cooking Time:** 4 to 6 hours

Minestra di Fagioli

Vegetarian Bean Soup from Italy

Make up your own mixture of beans, or buy one that's been
mixed for you. This hearty soup is a meal in itself!

1½ pounds mixed Dried Beans (4 cups)
10 cups Vegetarian Vegetable Stock (see page 77)
1 cup chopped Celery
1 cup chopped Onion
2 14½-ounce cans diced Tomatoes (with juice)
2 tablespoons dried Parsley Flakes
1 tablespoon dried Oregano
1 tablespoon dried Basil
1 tablespoon dried Marjoram
1 tablespoon dried Thyme
4 teaspoons minced fresh Garlic
1½ teaspoons Red Chili Pepper Flakes
2 tablespoons Worcestershire Sauce
1 teaspoon freshly ground Black Pepper
Salt to Taste

Cover the beans with boiling water and soak for 1 hour, then drain and rinse. Place the beans in a large
stock pot with all but the salt. Bring to a boil over medium-high heat, then reduce the
heat and simmer, with cover ajar, for 4-6 hours (or until tender) stirring occasionally. Taste and
add salt as desired. Makes 4 quarts.

Serving Size: 8 ounces   **Calories:** 93   **Total Fat:** Less than 1 gr. (8%)
Sat. Fat: Less than 1 gr.   **Cholesterol:** Less than 1 gr.
Sodium: 590 mgs.   **Carbohydrates:** 17.7 grams

Cajun Shrimp Soup

1½ tablespoons Butter
1½ tablespoons Olive Oil
¼ cup EACH chopped Sweet Red and Green Bell Pepper
1 cup chopped Onion
½ cup chopped Celery
2 teaspoons minced Garlic
2 tablespoons Flour
6 cups Water
2 Fish-flavored Bouillon Cubes
¼ cup chopped fresh Parsley
2 14½-ounce cans peeled and
diced Tomatoes (with juice)
2 tablespoons Worcestershire Sauce
¼ teaspoon Cayenne Pepper
1 teaspoon Paprika
2 Bay Leaves
2 teaspoons dried Thyme
½ cup Uncooked Long Grain Rice
2 pounds large Green (raw) Shrimp, peeled and deveined
Salt to taste

Melt the butter and olive oil in a large stock pot over medium heat. Sauté the peppers, onion, celery and garlic until limp. Remove from heat, and stir in the flour. Then add the water, bouillon cubes, parsley, tomatoes, Worcestershire, cayenne, paprika, bay leaves and thyme. Return to the stove and bring to a boil over medium heat, stirring occasionally. Reduce heat and simmer (uncovered) for 30 minutes. Add the rice and cook 30 minutes longer. Add the shrimp, and simmer for an additional 10 minutes. Remove from heat and let rest for 5 minutes before serving. Taste and add salt if desired. Makes 4 quarts.

Serving Size: 8 ounces   **Calories:** 137   **Total Fat:** 3.9 grams (26%)
Sat. Fat: 1.2 grams   **Cholesterol:** 95.2 mgs.
Sodium: 387 mgs.   **Carbohydrates:** 11.5 grams

Preparation time: 10 minutes   **Cooking Time:** 10 minutes

Lemon-Avocado Soup

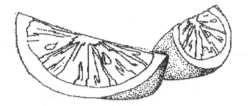

6 cups Chicken Broth
¼ cup chopped fresh Italian (flat-leaf) Parsley
½ cup Dry White Wine
¼ teaspoon coarse Sea Salt
1 Lemon, cut into 8, thin slices
1 large, ripe Avocado, peeled, seeded and thinly sliced

In a large saucepan, bring the chicken broth to a boil over medium heat. Add the parsley, wine and salt and simmer for 10 minutes. Divide the lemon and avocado slices equally between for soup bowls. Ladle in the hot broth. Serve immediately. Makes 2 quarts (8 servings).

Serving Size: 8 ounces   **Calories:** 82.4   **Total Fat:** 5 grams (52%)
Sat. Fat: Less than 1 gram   **Cholesterol:** 0 mgs.
Sodium: 653 mgs.   **Carbohydrates:** 3.4 grams

Preparation time: 30 minutes   **Cooking Time:** 1 hour and 20 minutes

Minestra di Pasta e Scarola

Italian Pasta and Escarole Soup with Chicken

1 tablespoon Extra Virgin Olive Oil
1 cup chopped Leeks
3 teaspoons minced Garlic
8 cups Chicken Broth
1 pound whole, boneless, skinless Chicken Thighs
1 14½-ounce can peeled and diced
Tomatoes, with juice
¼ cup chopped fresh Italian Parsley
2 teaspoons dried Marjoram Leaves
¼ teaspoon Red Pepper Flakes
½ teaspoon Salt
1 cup Rotini (or other large, shaped pasta...shells, tubetti, etc.)
4 cups coarsely chopped fresh Escarole or Curly Endive

❖

1 tablespoon freshly grated Peccorino-Romano Cheese per serving for garnish

In a large stock pot over medium heat, sauté the leeks and garlic in the olive oil until limp. Add the chicken broth, chicken thighs, tomatoes, parsley, marjoram, red pepper flakes and salt. Bring to a boil, then reduce the heat and simmer, uncovered, for 45 minutes to 1 hour, or until the chicken is very tender. Lift the chicken from the soup and let it cool for 5-10 minutes, or until cool enough to handle. Coarsely chop the meat and return it to the pot. Bring the soup back to a boil, and add the pasta. Cook for 10 minutes, then add the chopped escarole. Simmer for an additional 10 minutes. Taste and add extra salt, if desired. Serve hot, garnished with Peccorino-Romano. Makes 3½ quarts.

Serving Size: 8 ounces   **Calories:** 164   **Total Fat:** 7 grams (39%)
Sat. Fat: 2.5 grams   **Cholesterol:** 34.1 mgs.
Sodium: 714 mgs.   **Carbohydrates:** 9.5 grams

Preparation time: 30 minutes   **Cooking Time:** 45 minutes

Nouveau Bouillabaisse

French Fish Stew
A contemporary version of the classic.

1 cup chopped Onion
½ cup shredded Carrot
2 teaspoons minced Garlic
2 tablespoons Olive Oil
2 28-ounce cans Whole Peeled Tomatoes (with juice)
2 8-ounce bottles Clam Juice
1½ cups Dry White Wine
12 cups Water
½ teaspoon Fennel Seeds, crushed
1 teaspoon dried Thyme
1 large Bay Leaf
¼ cup chopped fresh Parsley
½ teaspoon Saffron Threads
1 teaspoon Salt
¼ teaspoon ground White Pepper
3 small Lobster Tails (5-6 ounces each), split in half lengthwise
¼ pound Dungeness Crab Meat (fresh or frozen)
½ pound EACH Red Snapper, Orange Roughy, and Cod filets, cut into 1" chunks
½ pound large Green (raw) Shrimp, peeled and deveined
12-14 fresh Mussels or Clams in the shell

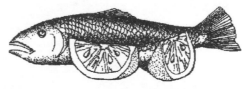

In a large stock pot over medium heat, sauté the onion, carrot and garlic in the olive oil until limp. Add the tomatoes, clam juice, white wine, water, herbs and seasonings, and bring the mixture to a full boil. Add the fish and seafood and bring the soup back to a boil. Reduce the heat and simmer for 30 minutes. Taste and add extra salt, if desired. Serve hot. Makes 6½ quarts.

Serving Size: 8 ounces   **Calories:** 98.6   **Total Fat:** 1.6 grams (15%)
Sat. Fat: Less than 1 gram   **Cholesterol:** 45.5 mgs.
Sodium: 407 mgs.   **Carbohydrates:** 4.6 grams

Oriental Chicken Soup

2 tablespoons Sesame Oil

3 slices fresh Ginger Root, about 1/8" thick

6 ounces boneless-skinless Chicken Breast Meat

6 ounces boneless-skinless Chicken Thighs

6 cups Chicken Broth

½ cup Rice Wine

1 tablespoon Soy Sauce

1 teaspoon Sugar

❖

2 Green Onions, thinly sliced, for garnish

Cut the chicken into slivers...set aside. In a wok or a large skillet, heat the sesame oil and stir-fry the ginger root until golden...about 1 minute. Remove and discard it. Immediately add the chicken breast and thigh meat and stir-fry for 5-7 minutes, or until lightly browned on all sides. Add the remaining ingredients and bring to a boil. (At this point, if you are using a skillet, you may need to transfer the meat to a stock pot to have room for the rest of the soup. If you do, be sure to scrape the pan to get all of the wonderful juices.)   Reduce the heat and simmer for 10 minutes. Ladle into bowls, and garnish with a teaspoon or so of the sliced green onion. Makes 2 quarts.

Serving Size: 8 ounces   **Calories:** 121   **Total Fat:** 5.6 grams (42%)
Sat. Fat: 1 gram   **Cholesterol:** 30 mgs.
Sodium: 743 mgs.   **Carbohydrates:** 1.6 grams

Preparation time: 30 minutes   **Cooking Time:** 1½ hours

Krupnik

Polish Vegetable Soup with Barley

2 tablespoons Olive Oil
1 cup chopped Onion
8 cups Beef Broth
¾ cup peeled, diced Carrot
1 cup peeled and diced Parsnip
1 cup sliced fresh Mushrooms
2 cups peeled and diced Russet Potatoes
½ cup chopped Celery
½ cup dry Pearled Barley
2 Bay Leaves
1 teaspoon Salt
½ teaspoon freshly ground Black Pepper

❖

1 teaspoon chopped fresh Dill Weed
(or ½ teaspoon dried Dill Weed) to garnish

In a large stock pot over medium heat, sauté the onion in the olive oil until limp. Add the remaining ingredients (except the dill weed) in the order given. Bring the soup to a boil. Reduce the heat, and simmer (uncovered) for 1 hour. Taste and add extra salt, if desired. Serve in bowls, garnished with dill weed. Makes 3 quarts.

Serving Size: 8 ounces   **Calories:** 100   **Total Fat:** 2.8 grams (25%)
Sat. Fat: Less than 1 gram   **Cholesterol:** 0 mgs.
Sodium: 710 mgs.   **Carbohydrates:** 15.5 grams

Preparation time: 30 minutes   **Cooking Time:** 45 minutes

Mediterranean Mussel Soup

2 tablespoons Extra Virgin Olive Oil
½ cup chopped Onion
½ cup chopped Celery
¼ cup shredded Carrot
3 teaspoons minced Garlic
2 tablespoons chopped fresh Basil
½ teaspoon Salt
¼ teaspoon freshly ground Black Pepper
1 cup Dry White Wine
6 cups Chicken Broth
2 14½-ounce cans peeled and diced Tomatoes
(with juice)
3 pounds fresh Mussels (in the shells)
¼ cup chopped fresh Parsley
Fresh Lemon Juice

In a Dutch oven over medium heat, sauté the onion, celery, carrot, garlic, basil, salt and pepper in the olive oil until limp. Add the wine, and reduce heat to simmer. Cook until liquid is reduced by half. Then, add the chicken broth and tomatoes. Bring to a boil over medium heat. Simmer (uncovered) for 30 minutes. Meanwhile, scrub the mussels with a stiff brush under cold, running water, removing their "beards" with a sharp knife. Discard any mussels that are open. Place the mussels in the pot with the other ingredients. Stir well, and bring back to a boil. Reduce heat and simmer (covered) for 10 minutes, or until all the mussels open. To serve, ladle soup into flat soup plates, and garnish with chopped parsley and a squeeze of fresh lemon juice. Makes 3 quarts.

Serving Size: 8 ounces   **Calories:** 97.3   **Total Fat:** 3.7 grams (34%)
Sat. Fat: Less than 1 gram   **Cholesterol:** 9.8 mgs.
Sodium: 649 mgs.   **Carbohydrates:** 5.9 grams

Preparation time: 10 minutes   **Cooking Time:** 2 hours

Tarragon Chicken Noodle Soup

1½-2 pounds Boneless-Skinless Chicken Thighs
12 cups Chicken Broth
1 cup chopped Onion
1 cup sliced Celery
½ cup Chopped fresh Parsley
1½ teaspoons dried Tarragon
(or 1 tablespoon fresh, chopped Tarragon)
¼ teaspoon ground Turmeric
½ teaspoon Salt
¼ teaspoon freshly ground Black Pepper
2 10-ounce packages frozen Chopped Spinach, defrosted
6 ounces dry, fine Egg Noodles

Put all the ingredients except the spinach and noodles in a large stock pot. Bring to a boil over medium-high heat. Reduce the heat, and simmer (uncovered) for 1½ hours, or until the chicken is very tender. With a slotted spoon, remove the chicken to a plate until cool the touch. Shred the meat back into the soup, discarding any bits of fat you might find. Just before serving, place the spinach in a colander and rinse well with cold water. Squeeze most of the moisture out of the spinach, and put it and the noodles into the soup. Bring to a boil, and cook approximately 10 minutes, or until the noodles are tender. Serve hot. Makes nearly 5 quarts.

Serving Size: 8 ounces   **Calories:** 164   **Total Fat:** 5.8 grams (32%)
Sat. Fat: 1.6 grams   **Cholesterol:** 43 mgs.
Sodium: 615 mgs.   **Carbohydrates:** 9.9 grams

Preparation time: 30 minutes **Chilling Time:** 2-4 hours

Andalusian Gazpacho

An authentic version of the Spanish classic!

½ cup diced Green Bell Pepper
½ cup diced Sweet Red Bell Pepper
1 cup chopped Onion
2 14½-ounce cans peeled and diced Tomatoes (with juice)
2 cups peeled and chopped Cucumbers
4 teaspoons minced Garlic
1 cup diced French bread cubes, without the crust

❖

2 tablespoons Tomato Paste
2 cups Spicy-Hot V-8® 100% Vegetable Juice
2 tablespoons Extra Virgin Olive Oil
¼ cup Red Wine Vinegar
1 tablespoon Paprika
1 teaspoon Salt
¼ teaspoon ground Cumin

For garnishing:
½ cup EACH sliced Green Onion Tops, Red, Green and Yellow Bell Pepper,
peeled and chopped Cucumber, and diced fresh Tomato

In the work bowl of a food processor fitted with a steel blade, purée the first seven ingredients. Place them in a large bowl, and stir in the next seven ingredients. Cover and refrigerate for several hours before serving. Taste and add extra salt, if desired. To serve, ladle soup into chilled bowls. Place the garnishes in several small bowls on the table and let your guests garnish the soup in their own fashion. A little Tabasco® sauce can add some extra zing! Your guests might like you to pass the bottle!
Makes 2½ quarts.

Serving Size: 8 ounces **Calories:** 100 **Total Fat:** 3.5 grams (29%)
Sat. Fat: Less than 1 gram **Cholesterol:** 0 mgs.
Sodium: 608 mgs. **Carbohydrates:** 16.3 grams

Cabbage Patch Soup

2 tablespoons Butter
1½ cups chopped Onion
1 cup sliced Celery
12 cups Vegetarian Vegetable Stock (see page 77)
(or 12 cups water mixed with 6 vegetarian vegetable bouillon cubes)
1 cup peeled and diced Carrots
1 cup peeled and diced Turnips
1 cup fresh or frozen Green Peas
1 cup peeled and diced Russet Potatoes
2 teaspoons minced Garlic
2 large Bay Leaves
2 tablespoons chopped fresh Basil
¼ cup chopped fresh Parsley
1 teaspoon Salt
½ teaspoon coarsely ground Black Pepper
2 tablespoons Worcestershire Sauce
Dash of Cayenne Pepper
8 large Tomatoes, peeled and diced
(or 2 14½-ounce cans peeled and diced Tomatoes, with juice)
1 cup chopped fresh Spinach
2 cups shredded Green Cabbage

In a large stock pot over medium heat, sauté the onion and celery in the butter until limp. Add the vegetarian vegetable stock, carrots, turnips, peas, potatoes, garlic, bay leaves, basil, parsley, salt, pepper, Worcestershire sauce and cayenne, and bring to a boil. Reduce the heat and simmer, uncovered for 40 minutes. Add the tomatoes, spinach and cabbage and simmer for an additional 20 minutes, or until the cabbage is very tender. Makes 5½ quarts.

Serving Size: 8 ounces   **Calories:** 65.1   **Total Fat:** 1.9 grams (25%)
Sat. Fat: Less than 1 gram   **Cholesterol:** 2.8 mgs.
Sodium: 270 mgs.   **Carbohydrates:** 11.5 grams

Preparation time: 30 minutes   **Cooking Time:** 1 hour

Minestrone Verde

"Green" Vegetable Soup from Italy

2 tablespoons Extra Virgin Olive Oil
2 cups sliced Leeks (white portion only)
1 cup sliced Celery
10 cups Chicken Broth
1 cup peeled and diced Turnip
1 cup peeled and diced Potato
1 cup fresh or frozen cut Green Beans
1 cup fresh or frozen Green Peas
1 15½-ounce can White (Great Northern) Beans
(with juice)
1 cup Cauliflower Flowerettes
½ cup chopped fresh Basil
3 teaspoons minced Garlic
1 teaspoon Salt
½ teaspoon freshly ground Black Pepper
1 cup Broccoli Flowerettes
1 cup chopped fresh Spinach
4 ounces Spaghetti (or Vermicelli) broken into 2" pieces

❖

1 tablespoon grated Parmesan per serving for garnish

In a large stock pot over medium-high heat, sauté the leeks and celery in the olive oil until limp. Add the chicken broth, turnip, potato, green beans, peas, white beans, cauliflower, basil, garlic, salt and pepper, and bring to a boil. Reduce the heat and simmer (uncovered) for 40 minutes. Add the broccoli, spinach and spaghetti and simmer for an addition 10 minutes. Serve hot, garnished with Parmesan.
Makes 4½ quarts.

Serving Size: 8 ounces   **Calories:** 145   **Total Fat:** 4.5 grams (28%)
Sat. Fat: 1.7 grams   **Cholesterol:** 4.9 mgs.
Sodium: 696 mgs.   **Carbohydrates:** 17.1 grams

Zupa Ogòrkowa

Polish Dill Pickle Soup

For the stock:
2 pounds Pork Bones (uncooked)
12 cups Water
1 whole Onion, peeled and quartered
1 large Carrot, peeled and cut into large chunks
2 large stalks Celery, cut into large chunks
1 large (or 2 small) Parsnips, peeled and cut into large chunks
12 Whole Black Peppercorns
1 teaspoon Whole Allspice
1 large Bay Leaf
1 teaspoon Salt

For the soup:
8 cups Stock (above)
5 large, whole Polish (brine-cured) Dill Pickles
2 cups peeled and diced Potatoes
2 tablespoons Dill Pickle Brine
¼ teaspoon freshly ground Black Pepper
¾ cup Sour Cream
2 tablespoons Flour

In a large stock pot over high heat, combine all the ingredients for the stock and bring to a boil. Reduce the heat, cover and simmer slowly, for 2 hours. As the stock cooks, skim the top, so as to produce a nice, clear broth. Refrigerate overnight. Skim the fat solids from the top of the soup. Strain the stock and discard the bones, vegetables and herbs. Return the stock to the pot. Peel and grate the dill pickles, and add them to the stock along with the potatoes, brine and black pepper. Bring to a boil, and then reduce the heat and simmer (uncovered) for 30 minutes. With a wire whisk, blend the sour cream and flour in a small bowl. Gradually add a ladle or two of the hot soup to raise the temperature of the sour cream. Stir the sour cream mixture into the soup. Bring back to a gentle simmer for 10 minutes. Taste and add salt or more brine as desired. Makes 2½ quarts.

Serving Size: 8 ounces **Calories:** 91.2 **Total Fat:** 4.2 grams (42%)
Sat. Fat: 2.2 grams **Cholesterol:** 14.2 mgs.
Sodium: 446 mgs. **Carbohydrates:** 11.1 grams

Hale and Hearty

Zuppa di Salsiccia

Italian Sausage Soup

1½-2 pounds Sweet Italian Sausage
1½ cups chopped Onion
3 teaspoons minced Garlic
1 cup chopped Sweet Red Bell Pepper
1½ cups shredded Cabbage
8 cups Chicken Broth
1 19-ounce can Fava Beans (with juice)
¼ cup chopped fresh Parsley
1 tablespoon dried Thyme
2 tablespoons dried Oregano
½ teaspoon freshly ground Black Pepper

In a large skillet, brown the sausage over medium-high heat, crumbling with a spoon. Meat should be fairly chunky. Drain and discard most of the fat, reserving about 1 tablespoon. Add the onion, garlic, red pepper and cabbage and sauté lightly, until vegetables are limp. Place the sautéed vegetables in a large stock pot with the remaining ingredients in the order given. Bring to a boil over medium-high heat. Reduce the heat and simmer, uncovered, for 1 hour. Serve hot. Makes 3½ quarts.

Serving Size: 8 ounces   **Calories:** 237   **Total Fat:** 15.4 grams (59%)
Sat. Fat: 5.4 grams   **Cholesterol:** 44.3 mgs.
Sodium: 1065 mgs.   **Carbohydrates:** 7.9 grams

Hungarian Cabbage Soup

3 tablespoons Butter
4 cups finely shredded Green Cabbage
1 cup peeled and shredded Apple
1 teaspoon minced Garlic
6 cups Chicken Broth
1 teaspoon Brown Sugar
½ teaspoon Caraway Seeds
½ teaspoon Salt
¼ teaspoon freshly ground Black Pepper

❖

For Spätzle:
(Note: 1½ cups of cooked dried spätzle or frozen
noodles may be substituted)
2/3 cup All Purpose White Flour
2 large Whole Eggs, beaten
1/4 teaspoon Salt
Additional Salt and freshly ground Black Pepper to taste

❖

Hungarian Sweet Paprika to garnish

In a large Dutch oven, melt the butter over medium heat and sauté the cabbage, apple and garlic until limp. Add the chicken broth, brown sugar, caraway seeds, salt and pepper. Raise the heat and bring to a boil. Reduce the heat and simmer (covered) for 30 minutes. Meanwhile, make the spätzle, by combining the flour, egg, and salt in a small bowl. Mix thoroughly with a fork. This will make a thick, sticky dough. When the soup is ready, drop the spätzle dough from the tip of a spoon in raisin-size bits into the simmering soup. Stir the soup occasionally, to keep the dumplings from sticking together. Let simmer for an additional 15 minutes. Dumplings will puff up to more than twice their size. Taste and add salt and pepper as desired. Ladle hot soup into bowls and garnish with a generous sprinkling of paprika. Makes 2+ quarts.

Serving Size: 8 ounces   **Calories:** 128   **Total Fat:** 6.1 grams (43%)
Sat. Fat: 3 grams   **Cholesterol:** 57.5 mgs.
Sodium: 754 mgs.   **Carbohydrates:** 12 grams

Beef Barley Soup

Don't let the number of ingredients in this recipe dissuade you from making this soul-satisfying soup... it's really very easy, and freezes very well, too!

2 pounds of Beef Stew Meat
1 tablespoon Olive Oil
1½ cup chopped Onion
8 cups Beef Broth
1½ cups chopped Sweet Red Bell Pepper
2 cups chopped Celery
2 cups diced Russet Potatoes (with peel)
2 cups coarsely shredded Cabbage
2 cups peeled and sliced Carrots
1 28-ounce can whole peeled Tomatoes
(chopped, with juice)
1 cup Dry Red Wine
(preferably a nice full-bodied Chianti)
2 tablespoons Worcestershire Sauce
½ teaspoon Dried Red Chili Pepper Flakes
½ cup chopped fresh Parsley
2 tablespoons dried Thyme
2 tablespoons dried Basil
2 large Bay Leaves
2 tablespoons mild Chili Powder
1 teaspoon coarsely ground Black Pepper
¾ cup medium Pearled Barley
Salt to taste

In a large stock pot, brown the beef in the olive oil over medium-high heat. When it is nicely browned on the outside, add the onions and sauté until translucent. Then add all but the last two ingredients in the order given. Bring to a boil and then reduce the heat and simmer for 2-3 hours, or until the meat is very tender. Next, add the barley and cook until it is tender...about 30 minutes. Taste and add salt if desired. Serve hot. Makes 5 quarts.

Serving Size: 8 ounces   **Calories:** 241   **Total Fat:** 10.7 grams (40%)   **Sat. Fat:** 4 grams   **Cholesterol:** 45 mgs.   **Sodium:** 668 mgs.   **Carbohydrates:** 18 gr.

All About Barley
An ancient and hardy grain, barley can be grown in most climates, where it is frequently used in the brewing of beer. "Pearled Barley" has the germ and the bran removed and contains more than 5 times the fiber than rice, and twice that of pasta*. If you cook pasta, you already know how to use barley...just substitute it in your favorite pasta dish for a nutritious and flavorful alternative. A staple in many middle-eastern countries, it's also a great source of protein.

* Based on 1 cup cooked single serving.

Reuben Soup

2 tablespoons Butter
¾ cup chopped Onion
½ cup chopped Celery
1 tablespoon Flour
4 cups Beef Broth
1 pound Sauerkraut, preferably fresh, but canned will do
¼ cup chopped fresh Parsley
½ pound thick sliced (1/8") Corned Beef, shredded

❖

3 slices Dark Rye Bread (Pumpernickel)
2 tablespoons Butter
1 cup shredded Swiss Cheese

In a large stock pot over medium heat, sauté the onion and celery in the butter until very tender, stirring frequently. Remove from heat and stir in the flour. Gradually add the beef broth, and return the pot to the stove. Add the sauerkraut, parsley and corned beef. Bring to a boil, then reduce the heat and simmer (covered) for 45 minutes. Cut the bread into 1½" to 2" cubes. In a large skillet over low-medium heat, sauté the bread cubes in the butter until they are crisp and well toasted, stirring constantly, being careful not to let them burn. To serve, ladle the soup into bowls and top with a few toasted bread cubes and about 2 tablespoons grated cheese. Place the soups in a preheated broiler for 1 minute, or until the cheese begins to lightly brown. Makes 2 quarts.

Serving Size: 8 ounces   **Calories:** 207   **Total Fat:** 13.9 grams (60%)
Sat. Fat: 7.1 grams   **Cholesterol:** 49.5 mgs.
Sodium: 1128 mgs.   **Carbohydrates:** 9.9 grams

Preparation time: 30minutes   **Cooking Time:** 45 minutes

Albòndigas

Mexican Meatball Soup

For the Meatballs:
½ pound lean ground Beef
½ pound ground Veal
2 large Whole Eggs
2 tablespoons minced Pimento
¼ cup finely chopped fresh Cilantro
2 teaspoons minced Garlic
½ teaspoon ground Cumin
½ teaspoon Salt
1/8 teaspoon freshly ground Black Pepper

❖

For the Soup:
8 cups Beef Broth
1 cup chopped Onion
1 cup peeled and ¼" diced Carrots
2 cups sliced Zucchine
1 cup shredded Green Cabbage
Salt to taste

Combine all of the meatball ingredients in a medium bowl, mixing thoroughly. Set aside. Bring the beef broth to a boil in a large stock pot over medium heat. Add the onion and carrots. Shape the meat mixture into 1" meatballs, and drop them into the boiling soup. Reduce the heat and simmer (uncovered) for 30 minutes. Add the zucchine and cabbage and return to a simmer for an additional 15 minutes. Taste and add salt as desired. Serve hot. Makes 3 quarts.

Serving Size: 8 ounces   **Calories:** 111   **Total Fat:** 5.4 grams (44%)
Sat. Fat: 1.9 grams   **Cholesterol:** 65.1 mgs.
Sodium: 687 mgs.   **Carbohydrates:** 3.3 grams

Preparation time: 30-40 minutes   Cooking Time: 1 hour

Vellutata di Carciofi con Polpettine di Vitello

Italian Cream of Artichoke Soup with Tiny Veal Meatballs
(A updated version of an old favorite we've served at Brannon's!)

1 tablespoon Butter
½ cup chopped Onion
2 8½-ounce cans Artichoke Hearts (in water), drained and coarsely chopped
¼ cup Flour
8 cups Chicken Broth
Dash of Ground White Pepper
Dash of Nutmeg
1 teaspoon Salt
½ cup Marsala Wine (or sherry)
1 cup Whipping Cream
2-3 tablespoons Gold Medal Wondra®, or enough to thicken as desired
½ cup chopped fresh Parsley, for garnish

❖

For the Meatballs:
1 pound ground Veal
2 large whole Eggs
2 teaspoons dried Basil
½ teaspoon Salt
¼ teaspoon White Pepper
½ teaspoon Garlic Powder
3 tablespoons Dry Bread Crumbs

In a large stock pot over medium heat, sauté the onions in the butter until limp. Add the artichoke hearts and stir well. Remove from heat and sprinkle the flour over the artichokes, stirring well. Gradually add the chicken broth, then the white pepper, nutmeg, salt and marsala. Bring to a boil, then reduce the heat and simmer for 30 minutes. Meanwhile, combine all the ingredients for the meatballs in a medium bowl. Moisten your hands and shape the meat mixture into tiny meatballs (about ¾" in diameter), dropping them one at a time into the simmering soup. Continue to simmer for an additional 20 minutes. Add the cream and bring back to a boil. Sprinkle the Wondra® over the soup and stir well. Let simmer for a minute or two before deciding whether to add more Wondra®. Serve hot, garnished with parsley. Makes 3+ quarts.

Serving Size: 8 ounces   Calories: 203   Total Fat: 11.5 grams (51%)
Sat. Fat: 6.1 grams   Cholesterol: 77.4 mgs.
Sodium: 697 mgs.   Carbohydrates: 9.3 grams

Preparation time: 30 minutes   **Cooking Time:** 3 hours

Barszcz

Polish Beet Soup
Unlike the Russian "Borscht" generally served cold in the United States, Barszcz is
served hot, and makes a rich and satisfying meal.

12 cups Water
2-3 pounds Pork Spareribs

❖

2 cups peeled and shredded fresh Beets
3 cups julienned fresh Beet Greens
3 tablespoons Flour
1 cup Sour Cream
2 tablespoons fresh Lemon Juice
1½ teaspoons Salt
Freshly ground Black Pepper to taste

❖

1 pound New Potatoes, (golfball-size, or smaller)

In a large stock pot over medium-high heat, bring the water and spareribs to a boil. Reduce the heat, and simmer, uncovered, for 1½-2 hours, or until the spareribs are very tender. Skim the top of the soup as it cooks, to produce a good, clear broth. Strain the broth and return it to the stock pot, reserving the meat and bones. Remove the meat from the bones and shred it...set aside. Discard the bones and fat. Measure the stock, and add enough water to make a total of 8 cups. Bring the stock to a boil again, and add the beets and greens. Reduce the heat and simmer, uncovered, for 20-30 minutes. Meanwhile, cook the new potatoes (in the skins) until tender...about 20-25 minutes...let cool, then slice. Set aside. In a small bowl, combine the flour and sour cream. Stir until well blended. Add a ladle or two of the broth to the sour cream to warm it, then stir it into the soup. Add the lemon juice, salt and pepper and heat thoroughly. Taste and adjust seasoning, if desired. To serve, ladle soup into bowls and serve with shredded meat and sliced potatoes. Makes 3+ quarts.

Serving Size: 8 ounces   **Calories:** 147   **Total Fat:** 9 grams (55%)
Sat. Fat: 4.1 grams   **Cholesterol:** 30.2 mgs.
Sodium: 249 mgs.   **Carbohydrates:** 9.5 grams

Preparation time: 30 minutes   **Cooking Time:** 2 hours

Basque Lamb Stew

2 Lamb Shanks (with bone), cut into 1" thick slices
1½ pounds Lamb Stew Meat, cut into 1" cubes
2 tablespoons Olive Oil
1 cup coarsely chopped Onion
2 teaspoons minced Garlic
6 cups Beef Broth
1 cup Dry Red Wine
2 tablespoons Tomato Paste
1½ teaspoons dried Rosemary
2 cups Carrots, peeled and cut diagonally into ¾" slices
1 cup fresh or frozen Whole Pearl Onions
(if fresh, onions should be peeled)
1 15½-ounce can White Beans, with juice
1 tablespoon fresh Lemon Juice
Salt and freshly ground Black Pepper to taste

❖

Grated Lemon Peel and chopped fresh Parsley to garnish

Your butcher can cut the lamb shanks for you. Heat the oil in a large Dutch oven over high heat until it begins to smoke. Add the lamb shanks and stew meat and brown quickly on all sides. Add the onion and garlic and reduce the heat to medium. Continue to sauté until the onion is limp. Then, add the remaining ingredients in the order given. Stir well. Cover and bring the stew back to a boil, stirring occasionally. Reduce the heat, and simmer (covered) for 1½ to 2 hours, or until the meat is very tender. To serve, ladle into flat soup plates and garnish with a little grated lemon peel and shopped parsley.
Makes 3½ quarts.

Serving Size: 11 ounces   **Calories:** 235   **Total Fat:** 10.3 grams (40%)
Sat. Fat: 3.8 grams   **Cholesterol:** 64.1 mgs.
Sodium: 497 mgs.   **Carbohydrates:** 11.5 grams

Preparation time: 30 minutes   **Cooking Time:** 45 minutes

Pallottoline in Brodo

Italian Meatball and Noodle Soup

For the Meatballs:
1 pound Extra Lean Ground Beef
2 whole Large Eggs, lightly beaten
½ cup minced Onion
¼ cup chopped fresh Parsley
1 teaspoon dried Oregano Leaves
1 teaspoon dried Basil
½ teaspoon dried Rosemary
1 teaspoon Garlic Powder
½ teaspoon Salt
¼ teaspoon freshly ground Black Pepper
1/3 cup dry Italian Bread Crumbs

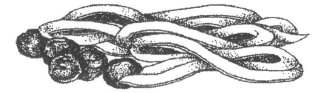

8 cups Beef Broth
1 pound fresh Spinach Fettucine
or 12 ounces dried Fettucine (any flavor)
1 tablespoon freshly grated Parmesan Cheese per
serving to garnish

Combine all the meatball ingredients in a large bowl, mixing well. Mixture should be slightly sticky to the touch. Place the beef broth in a large stock pot over high heat and bring to a boil. Moisten your hands with water, shaking off the excess. Shape the meat mixture into 1" meatballs, dropping them into the soup as you go. When all the meatballs are in the soup, reduce the heat to medium, and simmer, uncovered for 30 minutes. About 10 minutes before serving, drop in the pasta and cook until al' dente.
Serve, garnished with Parmesan. Makes 3 quarts.

Serving Size: 8 ounces   **Calories:** 192   **Total Fat:** 8 grams (39%)
Sat. Fat: 3 grams   **Cholesterol:** 84.5 mgs.
Sodium: 747 mgs.   **Carbohydrates:** 13.4 grams

Preparation time: 30 minutes   **Cooking Time:** 2½ hours

Hearty Beef and Squash Stew

2 tablespoons Olive Oil
1½ pounds Beef Stew Meat
1 cup chopped Onion
¼ cup Whiskey
2 teaspoons minced Garlic
½ cup chopped Green Bell Pepper
½ cup chopped Sweet Red Bell Pepper
8 cups Beef Broth
½ teaspoon freshly ground Black Pepper
1 teaspoon Salt
¼ cup A-1 Steak Sauce®
1 teaspoon grated fresh Ginger
1 6-ounce can Tomato Paste
1 15½-ounce can Great Northern Beans (with juice)
3 cups Butternut Squash (peeled and ½" diced)

In a large stock pot over high heat, sear the beef in the olive oil until nicely browned on all sides. Reduce the heat to medium and add the onion and sauté for 2-3 minutes, or until limp. Next, pour in the whiskey and stir constantly, until the liquid evaporates. Then, add the garlic, peppers (green and red), broth, pepper, salt, A-1®, ginger, and tomato paste. Bring the soup back to a boil, then reduce the heat and simmer slowly (covered) for 1½ hours, or until the beef begins to show signs of getting tender. Add the tomato paste, beans and squash and simmer for an additional hour. Taste, and add extra salt, if desired. Makes 4½ quarts.

Serving Size: 8 ounces   **Calories:** 201   **Total Fat:** 9.8 grams (43%)
Sat. Fat: 3.4 grams   **Cholesterol:** 37.8 mgs.
Sodium: 705 mgs.   **Carbohydrates:** 12.6 grams

Peasant Soup

A friend shared this recipe with me while I was a guest at her home in New York several years ago. The flavor was so wonderful, I embarrassed myself by eating at least 3 bowls that night...and that was the first time I'd met her! While it is a particularly time-consuming one to make...the result is well worth the effort!

2 veal shanks (about 2½ pounds each)
12 cups Water
4 teaspoons Salt
½ teaspoon freshly ground Black Pepper
¼ cup Olive Oil
½ cup chopped Celery
½ cup chopped fresh Spinach
½ cup chopped Green Pepper
½ cup chopped Onion
½ pound thinly sliced Pepperoni
2 cups peeled and diced Potatoes
2 cups peeled and diced Turnips or Rutabagas
2 cups peeled and diced Carrots
2 cups uncooked Macaroni Shells
1 1 lb. 14-ounce can of whole, peeled Tomatoes
1 10-ounce package frozen Peas
3¾ cups Beef Broth
1 teaspoon minced Garlic
½ teaspoon Dried Basil

❖

1 tablespoon freshly grated Parmesan cheese per serving to garnish.

Place the veal shanks in a large stock pot and add the water, 2 teaspoons of the salt, and ¼ teaspoon of the pepper. Cover and bring to a boil.

Reduce the heat and simmer for 2 hours. Remove the meat and bones from the stock. Remove the meat from the bones and chop coarsely. Place the meat in a covered container and refrigerate. Chill the stock over night. The next day, skim the fat from the top of the veal stock. Bring the stock to a simmer over medium heat. Meanwhile, in a large skillet, heat the olive oil, and sauté the celery, spinach, green pepper and onion until the onions begin to brown. Add the skillet contents to the veal broth...then the pepperoni, potatoes, turnips (or rutabagas) and carrots. Simmer until vegetables are <u>almost</u> tender (about 20 minutes).

Add the uncooked macaroni, chopped veal, tomatoes, peas, beef broth, remaining salt and pepper, garlic and basil. Simmer until shells are cooked (about 15 minutes). Serve hot, garnished with Parmesan.

Serving Size: 12 ounces **Calories:** 270 **Total Fat:** 11 grams (38%)
Sat. Fat: 3 grams **Cholesterol:** 88 mgs.
Sodium: 890 mgs. **Carbohydrates:** 15.5 grams

♥
Defatting Stock

Even canned stock can be made almost "Fat Free" by placing the can upright in the refrigerator over night. When you want to use the stock (broth), just open the can and skim the fat from the top. You'll get all the flavor...and essentially none of the fat!

Canèderli in Brodo

Savory dumplings in broth...a satisfying soup from Italy.

4 whole large Eggs, lightly beaten
1 cup Whole Milk
½ teaspoon Salt
4 cups stale Bread Cubes (preferable a mixture
of white, wheat and dark rye)
4 ounces Pancetta (Italian "bacon") or Bacon, finely diced
2 ounces Genoa Salami, finely diced
½ cup minced Onion
½ cup minced Celery
½ cup chopped fresh Parsley
¼ teaspoon freshly ground Black Pepper
½ cup grated Parmesan Cheese
1/3 cup All Purpose White Flour

❖

8 cups Beef Broth
1 tablespoon freshly grated Parmesan per serving for garnish

In a large bowl, beat together the eggs, milk and salt. Add the bread cubes combining well. Set aside for 20 minutes. Meanwhile, in a medium skillet, sauté the pancetta, salami, onion and celery until the vegetables are limp, and the bacon begins to brown. Remove from heat and add to the bread mixture. Then add the remaining ingredients (except the beef broth and cheese) and mix well. Mixture should be firm enough to form golf ball size dumplings. If mixture is too moist, add a little additional flour to bind the ingredients together. Shape into 12 dumplings (about 2-3 ounces each) and set aside. Bring the beef broth to a gentle boil in a large Dutch oven. Drop the dumplings into the broth one at a time, allowing the broth to return to a boil between additions. Simmer the dumplings (uncovered) for 15 minutes. Serve hot in flat soup plates garnished with the cheese. Makes 2½ quarts.

Serving Size: 8 ounces   **Calories:** 199   **Total Fat:** 11 grams (50%)
Sat. Fat: 4.3 grams   **Cholesterol:** 88.5 mgs.
Sodium: 1033 mgs.   **Carbohydrates:** 12.5 grams

Lattuga Ripiena in Brodo

A traditional Italian soup of beef-filled lettuce leaves in broth.

For the Lettuce Rolls:
½ tablespoon Olive Oil
2 pounds Beef Chuck Steak
2 cups Beef Broth
1 large Bay Leaf
Freshly ground Black Pepper to taste
2 whole Large Eggs, lightly beaten
½ cup freshly grated Parmesan
¼ cup chopped fresh Parsley

❖

8 large Romaine Lettuce Leaves
4 Cups Beef Broth

❖

For the Pesto Sauce:
2 cups fresh Basil Leaves
½ cup chopped fresh Parsley
½ cup freshly grated Parmesan Cheese
4 teaspoons minced fresh Garlic
1 teaspoon Pignoli (Pine Nuts)
¾ cup Extra Virgin Olive Oil

In a pressure cooker over medium-high heat, sear the beef in the olive oil until well browned. Add the 2 cups of beef broth, the bay leaf and black pepper. Cover and seal the pressure cooker and process according to manufacturer's directions for 30 minutes. Run cold water over the pressure cooker to cool it, until the safety valve drops, indicating that the pressure in the pan has been released. Open the pan and remove the beef to a plate to cool, reserving the cooking liquid. When cool enough to handle, shred the beef into a medium bowl. Add the eggs, cheese and parsley, mixing well. Set aside. Bring a large stock pot of water to a boil over high heat. Drop the lettuce leaves into the boiling water and remove the pot from the heat. Let stand for 3 minutes. Drain the lettuce leaves, and cool them under running water. Pat dry with paper towels, and spread the leaves out onto a clean, dry countertop. Distribute the meat mixture evenly between the eight leaves, and roll each one up, "egg-roll" style. Secure each roll with a wooden toothpick and set them aside. Next, make the pesto sauce. Place all the pesto sauce ingredients in the work bowl of a food processor fitted with a steel blade. Process by pulsing the machine, until the mixture is well blended, scraping down the sides of the work bowl as needed. Place the reserved cooking liquid and the 4 cups of additional beef broth in a large skillet with the lettuce rolls. Bring to a boil over medium heat and simmer, covered, for 15 minutes. Serve the rolls hot with a little of the broth...topped with a teaspoon of the pesto sauce. Makes 8 servings.

Serving Size: 8 ounces   Calories: 356   Total Fat: 19.6 grams (51%)
Sat. Fat: 7.8 grams   Cholesterol: 178 mgs.
Sodium: 805 mgs.   Carbohydrates: 1 gram

♥
Pressure Cookers
You don't hear much about pressure cookers today, but the new ones are safe to use, and they tenderize meat in a fraction of the time! Simmering meat on top of the stove is an acceptable alternative, but it won't produce as good a result as a pressure cooker!

Preparation time: 30 minutes   **Cooking Time:** 1 hour

Minestrone con Polpettine

Italian Minestrone with Meatballs

2 tablespoons Olive Oil
1 cup coarsely chopped fresh Onion
2 teaspoons minced fresh Garlic
4 ounces sliced fresh Mushrooms
8 cups Beef Broth
2 14½-ounce cans peeled and diced Tomatoes
(with juice)
2 15½-ounce cans Great Northern Beans
(with juice)
2 cups sliced Zucchini
1 10-ounce package frozen Spinach
1 9-ounce package frozen Artichoke Hearts
½ cup chopped fresh Basil
(or 2 tablespoons dried)
2 tablespoons chopped fresh Oregano
(or 1 tablespoon dried)
½ teaspoon freshly ground Black Pepper
1 teaspoon Salt
2 tablespoons Worcestershire Sauce
8 ounces dried Spaghetti, broken into 2" lengths
1 tablespoon grated Parmesan per serving

❖

For the Meatballs:
1 pound Hot or Sweet Italian Sausage
2 large whole Eggs, lightly beaten
¼ teaspoon Garlic Powder
1 teaspoon dried Oregano
2 tablespoons finely minced fresh Onion
1 tablespoon chopped fresh Parsley
¼ cup Dry Bread Crumbs

In a large stock pot over medium-high heat, sauté the onion and garlic in the olive oil until limp. Add the mushrooms and continue to sauté until they begin to lightly brown. Add the broth, tomatoes, great northern beans, zucchini, spinach, artichoke hearts, basil, oregano, pepper, salt and Worcestershire sauce. Bring to a boil...then reduce the heat and simmer (uncovered) for 30 minutes. Meanwhile, combine all the ingredients for the meatballs in a large bowl. Mix well with your hands. Shape the mixture into 1" meatballs and drop them into the soup. (Lightly wetting your hands several times during this process will keep the meat mixture from sticking to your hands.) Bring the soup back to a simmer, and cook for 15 minutes. Add the spaghetti and cook 15 minutes more. Serve hot, garnished with Parmesan. Makes 6 quarts.

Serving Size: 8 ounces **Calories:** 220 **Total Fat:** 10.1 grams (41%)
Sat. Fat: 3.8 grams **Cholesterol:** 36.9 mgs.
Sodium: 707 mgs. **Carbohydrates:** 21 grams

❤

"Minestrone" is a variation of the Italian word "minestra". Just as "gamberetti" means little shrimp and "gamberoni" means large shrimp or prawns, "minestrone" means "big soup", or one that is a meal in itself. There are hundreds of recipes for "minestrone", but all follow some basic guidelines:

a) they are jam packed with vegetables
b) they all include some form of pasta
c) all are garnished with grated cheese

Preparation time: 15-20 minutes   **Cooking Time:** 45 minutes

Salmon Chowder

2 tablespoons Butter
1 cup chopped fresh Onion
¾ cup sliced Celery
8 cups Chicken Broth
½ cup chopped fresh Parsley
1 14½-ounce can peeled and diced Tomatoes (drained)
2 cups fresh or frozen Corn
2 cups peeled and diced Russet Potatoes
1 teaspoon dried Thyme
¼ teaspoon ground White Pepper
1 teaspoon Salt
1 cup Heavy Whipping Cream
2 tablespoons Flour
1-1½ pounds fresh Salmon Filets, rinsed
2 tablespoons Lemon Juice

❖

Chopped fresh Parsley to garnish

In a large stock pot over medium-high heat, sauté the onion and celery in the butter until limp...about 5 minutes. Add the chicken broth, parsley, tomatoes, corn, potatoes, thyme, pepper and salt. Bring the soup back to a boil, then reduce the heat and simmer, uncovered, for 30 minutes. In a small bowl, whisk together the cream and flour...then stir it into the soup. Cut the salmon filets into 1" cubes, making sure to remove all bones. Add the salmon and the lemon juice to the soup and simmer for 15-20 minutes, stirring occasionally. Serve hot, garnished with chopped parsley. Makes 4½ quarts.

Serving Size: 8 ounces   **Calories:** 184   **Total Fat:** 11.1 grams (54%)
Sat. Fat: 5.0 grams   **Cholesterol:** 46.6 mgs.
Sodium: 546 mgs.   **Carbohydrates:** 9.9 grams

Preparation time: 15-20 minutes   **Cooking Time:** 1 hour and 10 minutes

Cream of Cauliflower Soup au Gratin

2 tablespoons Butter
½ cup coarsely chopped Onion
1 cup shredded Cabbage
8 cups Chicken Broth
1 teaspoon Salt
¼ teaspoon ground White Pepper
3 cups Cauliflower Flowerettes
¾ cup uncooked Long Grain Rice
1 cup Heavy Whipping Cream
2 tablespoons Flour

❖

1 cup shredded Swiss Cheese for garnish

In a large stock pot over medium heat, sauté the onion and cabbage in the butter until wilted. Add the chicken broth, salt, and white pepper. Bring to a boil...then reduce the heat and simmer (uncovered) for 30 minutes. Add the cauliflower and rice and simmer an additional 30 minutes, or until the rice is tender. In a small bowl, whisk the whipping cream with the flour to remove all lumps. Stir the cream into the soup and return it to a boil. Simmer for 10 minutes more. To serve, ladle into bowls and top with grated Swiss cheese. Place under a broiler for 1-2 minutes, or until the cheese is melted. Makes 3 quarts.

Serving Size: 8 ounces   **Calories:** 202   **Total Fat:** 12.8 grams (57%)
Sat. Fat: 7.7 grams   **Cholesterol:** 40.6 mgs.
Sodium: 755 mgs.   **Carbohydrates:** 13.9 grams

Best of the Broths

Preparation time: 15 minutes   **Cooking Time:** 1 hour

Vegetarian Vegetable Stock

2 large Carrots, peeled and cut into chunks
1 large Onion, peeled and cut into chunks
4 large Celery Stalks
2 large Turnips, peeled and cut into chunks
2 large Leeks, washed and cut into chunks
2 large Parsnips, peeled and cut into chunks
4 whole cloves of Garlic
12 sprigs of fresh Parsley
3 Bay Leaves
1 teaspoon dried Thyme
1½ teaspoons Salt
½ teaspoon Whole Black Peppercorns
12 cups Water

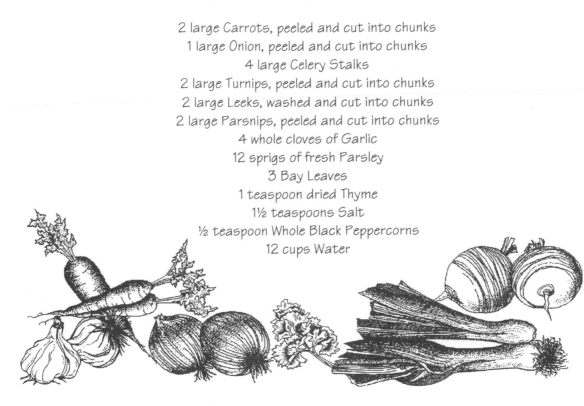

Combine all the ingredients in a large stock pot and bring to a boil, skimming the surface for a nice, clear broth. Simmer, covered, for 1 hour. Strain the stock and discard the vegetables. Let cool, then store in the refrigerator, or freezer, in a covered, plastic container. Use this tasty stock in any recipe that calls for Vegetable Broth (or vegetable bouillon + water), or Root Vegetable Stock. Also, use this stock to convert other vegetable based soups to total vegetarian. You'll greatly reduce the amount of fat, saturated fat, and cholesterol...without sacrificing the flavor!
Makes 2½ quarts.

Serving Size: 8 ounces   **Calories:** 31   **Total Fat:** Less than 1 gram (5%)
Sat. Fat: Less than 1 gram   **Cholesterol:** 0 mgs.
Sodium: 203 mgs.   **Carbohydrates:** 5.6 grams

Preparation time: 15 minutes   **Cooking Time:** 2 hours + overnight to defat

Beef Stock

5 pounds Beef Bones
3 large Carrots, peeled and cut into chunks
3 large stalks of Celery, cut into chunks
1 large Onion, peeled and cut into chunks
6 whole cloves of Garlic
12 sprigs of fresh Parsley
3 Bay Leaves
1 teaspoon dried Thyme
1½ teaspoons Salt
1 teaspoon Whole Black Peppercorns
12 cups Water

Combine all the ingredients in a large stock pot and bring to a boil, skimming the surface for a nice, clear broth. Simmer, covered, for 2 hours. Strain the stock and discard the solids. Let cool, then refrigerate overnight in a covered, plastic container. The next day, skim excess fat from the surface of the stock, and discard. Use this tasty stock in any recipe that calls for Beef Broth or Beef Stock.

Makes 2½-3 quarts.

Serving Size: 8 ounces   **Calories:** 40   **Total Fat:** 1.3 grams (28%)
Sat. Fat: Less than 1 gram   **Cholesterol:** 10 mgs.
Sodium: 203 mgs.   **Carbohydrates:** 5.6 grams

Preparation time: 15 minutes   **Cooking Time:** 2 hours + overnight to defat

Chicken Stock

5 pounds boney Chicken Parts (backs, necks, wings)
2 large Carrots, peeled and cut into chunks
1 large Onion, peeled and cut into chunks
4 whole cloves of Garlic
12 sprigs of fresh Parsley
3 Bay Leaves
1 teaspoon dried Thyme
1½ teaspoons Salt
½ teaspoon Whole Black Peppercorns
12 cups Water

Combine all the ingredients in a large stock pot and bring to a boil, skimming the surface for a nice, clear broth. Simmer, covered, for 2 hours. Strain the stock and discard the solids. Let cool, then refrigerate overnight in a covered, plastic container. The next day, skim excess fat from the surface of the stock, and discard. Use this tasty stock in any recipe that calls for Chicken Broth or Chicken Stock.
Makes 2½-3 quarts.

Serving Size: 8 ounces   **Calories:** 40   **Total Fat:** 1.3 grams (28%)
Sat. Fat: Less than 1 gram   **Cholesterol:** 10 mgs.
Sodium: 203 mgs.   **Carbohydrates:** 5.6 grams

Preparation time: 30 minutes   **Cooking Time:** 1½ hours

Fritattine in Brodo

Italian Omelet "Noodles" in a Flavorful Broth

For the Broth;
8 cups Chicken Broth
2 14½-ounce cans diced Tomatoes (with juice)
1 tablespoon dried Oregano
1 tablespoon dried Basil
2 teaspoons dried Thyme
¼ cup fresh chopped Parsley
½ teaspoon freshly ground Black Pepper
Salt to taste

❖

For the Fritattine:
12 whole Extra Large Eggs, well beaten
1 teaspoon EACH, Oregano, Basil and Thyme
Dash of Salt
1/8 teaspoon freshly ground Black Pepper

❖

1 tablespoon freshly grated
Parmesan Cheese per serving for garnish

Combine all the ingredients for the broth in a large stock pot. Bring to a boil. Reduce the heat and simmer, uncovered, for 1 hour. Meanwhile, make the "noodles" by combining all of the ingredients in a medium bowl. Heat a 10" Teflon®-coated omelet pan over medium-high heat. Coat the pan with non-stick vegetable spray. Place ¼ cup of the egg mixture into the pan, quickly swirling to coat the entire bottom of the pan. Let bake for 1-2 minutes, or until the edges of the omelet begin to curl and lightly brown. Using a pancake turner, turn the omelet and bake on the other side for 30 seconds.

Remove the omelet from the pan and place on a clean dry countertop to cool, while you make the remaining omelets. Stack them up and cut them into thin noodles. Just before serving, add them to the broth and simmer for 15 to 20 minutes. Serve hot, garnished with Parmesan. Makes 3½ quarts.

Serving Size: 8 ounces   **Calories:** 139   **Total Fat:** 7.8 grams (51%)
Sat. Fat: 3 grams   **Cholesterol:** 216 mgs.
Sodium: 871 mgs.   **Carbohydrates:** 4.5 grams

Preparation time: 30 minutes   **Cooking Time:** 1½ hours

Chicken Soup with Wild Rice

1 tablespoon Olive Oil
1 cup coarsely chopped Onion
1 cup chopped Celery
½ cup shredded Carrot
1½ cups thinly sliced fresh Mushrooms
(about ½ pound)
8 cups Chicken Broth
1 cup Wild Rice
½ cup chopped fresh Parsley
½ teaspoon freshly ground Black Pepper
2 teaspoons ground or rubbed Sage
1 teaspoon dried Marjoram
1 teaspoon Salt
3-3½ pounds split Chicken Breasts (including skin and breast bones)
½ cup Dry Vermouth

In a large stock pot over medium heat, sauté the onion, celery, carrot and mushrooms in the olive oil until tender. Stir in the chicken broth and bring the soup to a boil. Add the wild rice, parsley , pepper, sage, marjoram, salt and chicken breasts and return to a boil. Reduce the heat and simmer, covered, for 1 hour. Remove the breasts from the soup and let cool for 5-10 minutes, or until cool enough to handle. Remove the skin and bones from the chicken and discard. Dice the breast meat and return it to the soup. Bring the soup back up to a boil and add the vermouth. Simmer for 10 minutes. Taste and season with additional salt, if desired. Makes 4½ quarts.

Serving Size: 8 ounces   **Calories:** 150   **Total Fat:** 4.5 grams (27%)
Sat. Fat: 1.1 grams   **Cholesterol:** 28.4 mgs.
Sodium: 498 mgs.   **Carbohydrates:** 10.9 grams

French Onion Soup Gratinée

The classic method. The best flavor!

2 tablespoons Butter
2 tablespoons Extra Virgin Olive Oil
8 cups thinly sliced Onion
1 teaspoon Sugar
½ teaspoon Salt
2 tablespoons Flour
8 cups Beef Broth
2 cups French Vermouth (or dry white wine)
Salt and freshly ground Black Pepper to taste

❖

1 large loaf of crisp French Bread
4 ounces thinly sliced Swiss Cheese
¼ cup Cognac
8 tablespoons (about 2 oz.) grated Swiss Cheese
8 tablespoons (about 2 oz.) grated Parmesan
Freshly ground Black Pepper to taste

❖

2 Egg Yolks, well beaten
¼ cup Port Wine

For the soup: In a large stock pot over medium heat, sauté the onions in the butter and olive oil until tender (about 20 minutes). Add the sugar and salt, and raise the heat to medium-high and continue sautéing for about 35-40 minutes, or until the onions caramelize, and turn very soft. (This will yield a little more than 1 cup when they are caramelized.)   Remove from the heat, and stir in the flour, until well blended. Gradually add the beef broth and vermouth. Return to medium heat, and bring the soup to a slow simmer. Taste and add salt and black pepper as desired. Meanwhile, cut the French bread into ¼" to ½"

thick rounds. Spread them in a single layer on a baking sheet and place them in a preheated 450° oven until crisp and golden brown, turning several times. This will take about 10 minutes, depending on your particular oven. Combine the grated cheeses, and set aside. **To serve the soup:** Butter individual oven-proof soup crocks, and line them with 2 or 3 bread rounds, and a slice or two of the Swiss cheese.   Ladle in the simmering soup, and float 2 or 3 of the bread rounds on top. Sprinkle 2 tablespoons of the grated cheeses onto the bread rounds, and top with a grinding of pepper. Place the soup crocks on a sturdy baking tray and bake them in a 425° oven for about 20 minutes, or until they are nicely browned on top. Remove from the oven and set aside. Whisk together the egg yolks and the Port wine in a small bowl. Just before serving, lift a side of the topping with a fork, and slip in a tablespoon of the egg/Port mixture... stirring underneath the crust with a spoon to lightly blend. Serve hot, before the crust sinks! Makes 3½ quarts.

Serving Size: 8 ounces + toppings   **Calories:** 240   **Total Fat:** 8.6 grams (32%)
Sat. Fat: 4.1 grams   **Cholesterol:** 42.4 mgs.
Sodium: 762 mgs.   **Carbohydrates:** 21.6 grams

To pick the sweetest onion, always pick the one with the **thickest** layers. Thin layers indicate sparse watering while the onion was growing, and will produce a much hotter onion.

Preparation time: 15 minutes   **Cooking Time:** 10 minutes

Dragon Whisker Soup

Chinese Meatball Soup

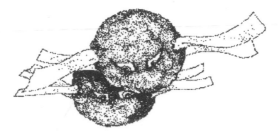

4 cups Chicken Broth
1/8 teaspoon Chinese Five Spice Powder
½ pound fresh Ground Pork (unseasoned)
1 whole large Egg
½ cup Dry Bread Crumbs
2 tablespoons Soy Sauce
1 tablespoon chopped fresh Parsley
2 Egg Roll Wrappers
3 Green Onions

In a large stock pot, heat the chicken broth and the Chinese five spices to boiling over medium-high heat. Meanwhile, combine the pork, egg, bread crumbs, soy sauce and parsley...mixing well. Fold the egg roll wrappers into thirds and with a sharp knife, cut them into ¼" wide noodles...or "whiskers". Shape the meat mixture into 1" meatballs ("dragons"), wrapping the meat around the middle of two of the "whiskers", leaving the ends dangling out of either side. Drop the "dragons" into the boiling soup, and simmer for 8-10 minutes. Serve hot, garnished with thin slices of green onion. Makes 1½ quarts.

Serving Size: 8 ounces   **Calories:** 201   **Total Fat:** 10 grams (47%)
Sat. Fat: 3.6 grams   **Cholesterol:** 71 mgs.
Sodium: 925 mgs.   **Carbohydrates:** 10 grams

Preparation time: 30 minutes   **Cooking Time:** 2½-3 hours

Cock-a-Leekie

An old Scottish recipe for chicken soup flavored with leeks.

1 large Stewing Hen, about 4 pounds
8 cups Chicken Broth
4 Whole Cloves
1 teaspoon ground Mace
1 teaspoon Salt
6 Whole Black Peppercorns
3 cups chopped Leeks (white portion only)
1½ cups uncooked Long Grain Rice (long cooking type)
10-12 Whole Pitted Prunes

In a large stock pot over medium-high heat, bring the hen, broth, cloves, mace, salt and peppercorns to a boil. Reduce the heat and simmer, covered, 2 hours, or until the chicken is very tender. Skim the top of the soup as it cooks, to produce a lovely, clear broth. When tender, remove the hen from the broth and set aside until cool to the touch. Meanwhile, strain the broth, and return it to the pot. Add the leeks, rice and prunes. Return to a simmer and cook (uncovered) for 30 minutes, or until the rice is tender. While the soup is cooking, bone the chicken, discarding the skin, fat and bones. Cut the meat into large chunks, and add it to the soup. Bring the soup back to a simmer. Serve hot.

Makes 3½ quarts.

Serving Size: 8 ounces   **Calories:** 309   **Total Fat:** 13.3 grams (40%)
Sat. Fat: 3.6 grams   **Cholesterol:** 51.1 mgs.
Sodium: 649 mgs.   **Carbohydrates:** 23.7 grams

Scandinavian Eggplant Soup

3 cups peeled and 1" diced Eggplant (1 large or 2 small)
1 tablespoon Coarse Salt
¼ cup Extra Virgin Olive Oil
1 cup finely chopped Onion
½ cup EACH, finely diced Carrot and Celery
1 teaspoon minced Garlic
½ teaspoon ground Coriander
¼ teaspoon ground Cumin
½ teaspoon dried Thyme
1/8 teaspoon Cinnamon
1/8 teaspoon freshly ground Black Pepper
½ cup chopped fresh Parsley
8 cups Water + 4 Vegetarian Bouillon Cubes
OR 8 cups Vegetarian Vegetable Stock (see page 77)
Salt to taste

❖

2/3 cup Sour Cream and
Chopped fresh parsley to garnish

Place the diced eggplant in a large colander and sprinkle with the coarse salt. Set aside for 30 minutes, and allow to drain. In a large stock pot over medium-high heat, sauté the onion, carrot, celery and garlic in the olive oil until limp. Rinse the eggplant well under running water. Add the eggplant and the herbs and spices...tossing to coat well . Add the water and the bouillon cubes and bring to a boil. Reduce heat and simmer for 1 hour. Taste and add salt, if desired.   Ladle into individual bowls and top with a tablespoon of sour cream and a sprinkling of parsley. Serve hot. Makes nearly 3 quarts.

Serving Size: 8 ounces   **Calories:** 105   **Total Fat:** 8.1 grams (68%)
Sat. Fat: 2.6 grams   **Cholesterol:** 6.3 mgs.
Sodium: 431 mgs.   **Carbohydrates:** 7.1 grams

Wonton Soup

For the wontons;
½ pound fresh Ground Pork (unseasoned)
1 large Whole Egg, lightly beaten
1½ tablespoons Soy Sauce
½ cup dry Bread Crumbs
16-18 Wonton Skins
2 Egg Yolks, lightly beaten

❖

For the broth:
6 cups Chicken Broth
1/8 teaspoon Chinese Five Spice Powder
1 tablespoon Soy Sauce
3/4 cup fresh Snow Peas, stems removed
2 large Green Onions, sliced (including tops)

Combine the pork, whole egg, soy sauce and bread crumbs, mixing thoroughly. Shape into 1" balls. Place 1 ball in the center of each wonton skin. Brush the beaten egg yolk onto the wonton skin, coating about ¼" in from the edge. Fold the wontons in half diagonally (sealing them) and set them aside. In a large stock pot, bring the chicken broth to a boil over high heat. Add the Chinese five spice powder, and the soy sauce. Reduce the heat to a moderate boil, and cook, uncovered for 10 minutes. Drop the wontons into the simmering soup, one at a time. Simmer for 10 minutes more. Just before serving, add the snow peas and green onions. Serve hot. Makes 2 quarts.

Serving Size: 8 ounces   **Calories:** 219   **Total Fat:** 8 grams (34%)
Sat. Fat: 2.7 grams   **Cholesterol:** 73.2 mgs.
Sodium: 961 mgs.   **Carbohydrates:** 20.6 grams

Preparation time: 20-30 minutes   **Cooking Time:** 1 hour

Succotash Soup

1 tablespoon Butter
1 cup chopped Onion
1 cup chopped Celery
2 teaspoons minced Garlic
8 cups Chicken Broth
1 16-ounce package frozen Baby Lima Beans
1 16-ounce package frozen Corn
1 meaty Smoked Ham Hock (or 1 cup diced Ham)
½ pound smoked Polish Sausage,
cut diagonally into ½" thick chunks
½ cup minced fresh Parsley
1 teaspoon ground Sage
½ teaspoon freshly ground Black Pepper
½ teaspoon Salt

In a large stock pot over medium heat, sauté the onion, celery and garlic in the butter until limp. Add the chicken broth, and then the remaining ingredients in the order given. Bring the soup to a boil. Reduce the heat and simmer (partially covered) for 1 hour. Lift the ham hock from the soup and let cool for 5-10 minutes, or until cool enough to handle. Remove the meat from the bones and chop coarsely. Discard the skin and bones, and add the chopped meat to the soup. Bring back to a simmer. Taste and add extra salt, if desired. Serve hot. Makes nearly 4 quarts.

Serving Size: 8 ounces   **Calories:** 172   **Total Fat:** 8.4 grams (43%)
Sat. Fat: 3.1 grams   **Cholesterol:** 22.8 mgs.
Sodium: 673 mgs.   **Carbohydrates:** 14.4 grams

Mediterranean Lamb Soup with Grilled Vegetables

2 Sweet Red Bell Peppers, cored, seeded and cut lengthwise into quarters
1 Sweet Yellow or Orange Bell Pepper, cored, seeded and cut lengthwise into quarters
6 slices of peeled Eggplant, each about ½" thick
2 small Zucchine (about ½ pound total), cut into long slices about ¼" thick
1 large Red Onion, cut into ½" thick slices
2 tablespoons Olive Oil
2 pounds Lamb Sirloin, cut into 1" chunks
2 teaspoons minced Garlic
1 tablespoon chopped fresh Oregano
½ cup chopped fresh Basil
2 14½-ounce cans peeled and diced Tomatoes (with juice)
8 cups Beef Broth
Salt and freshly ground Black Pepper to taste

Preheat a grill (or broiler) to very hot. Grill the peppers (skin side down), until the skins are blistered and blackened. Wrap them in a towel and set them aside. Spray the eggplant, zucchine and red onion slices with non-stick vegetable spray, then grill them until slightly limp and nicely browned. Set aside. In a large stock pot over medium-high heat, quickly brown the lamb on all sides. Add the garlic, oregano, basil, tomatoes and beef broth. Bring to a boil. Meanwhile, peel the peppers, and chop them coarsely. Coarsely chop the other vegetables, and add them to the soup. Simmer (partially covered) for 1 hour, or until the lamb is very tender. Taste and add salt and pepper as desired. Makes 4 quarts.

Serving Size: 8 ounces   **Calories:** 164   **Total Fat:** 7.1 grams (39%)
Sat. Fat: 2.2 grams   **Cholesterol:** 61.2 mgs.
Sodium: 566 mgs.   **Carbohydrates:** 3.5 grams

Preparation time: 15-20 minutes   **Cooking Time:** Less than 1 hour

Bavarian Smoked Sausage Soup

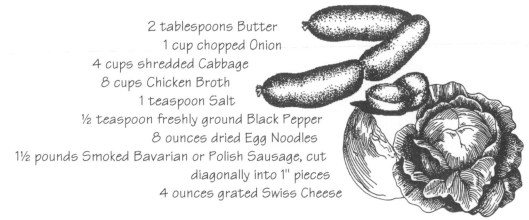

2 tablespoons Butter
1 cup chopped Onion
4 cups shredded Cabbage
8 cups Chicken Broth
1 teaspoon Salt
½ teaspoon freshly ground Black Pepper
8 ounces dried Egg Noodles
1½ pounds Smoked Bavarian or Polish Sausage, cut
diagonally into 1" pieces
4 ounces grated Swiss Cheese

In a large stock pot over medium-high heat, sauté the onion in the butter until limp. Add the shredded cabbage and continue to sauté until the cabbage begins to wilt. Add the chicken broth, salt and pepper and bring the soup to a boil. Reduce the heat and simmer, uncovered, for 30 minutes. Add the egg noodles and sausage and cook 10-15 minutes longer, or until the noodles are tender. To serve, ladle soup into bowls and garnish with a little grated Swiss cheese. Serve hot. Makes 4 quarts.

Serving Size: 8 ounces   **Calories:** 248   **Total Fat:** 4 grams (62%)
Sat. Fat: 6.9 grams   **Cholesterol:** 50.7 mgs.
Sodium: 931 mgs.   **Carbohydrates:** 11.2 grams

Preparation time: 20-30 minutes   **Cooking Time:** 30 minutes

Zuppa di Accia

Italian Egg and Sausage Soup

1-1½ pounds Sweet Italian Sausage
8 cups Beef Broth
4 cups Celery, cut diagonally into 1" pieces
8 rounds (approx. 3" in diameter) crusty French Bread, toasted
¼ pound Sopressata (or Genoa Salami), cut into julienne strips
4 Hard Boiled Eggs, peeled and quartered

❖

Freshly ground Black Pepper to taste
1 cup freshly grated Peccorino-Romano Cheese (or Parmesan)

In a large stock pot, brown the sausage over high heat, crumbling into small chunks as it cooks. Drain most all of the fat and discard. Add the beef broth, and bring the soup to a boil. Next, add the celery. Reduce the heat and simmer for 30 minutes, or until the celery is tender. To serve, place a toast round in the bottom of a flat soup plate. Top with a little salami, then two quarters of the hard boiled egg. Ladle boiling celery and broth over the top. Sprinkle on the grated cheese, and top with a grinding or two of black pepper. Serve immediately. Makes 2 quarts.

Serving Size: 8 ounces   **Calories:** 285   **Total Fat:** 19.8 grams (63%)
Sat. Fat: 7.5 grams   **Cholesterol:** 95.8 mgs.
Sodium: 1127 mgs.   **Carbohydrates:** 11 grams

Preparation time: 30 minutes   **Cooking Time:** 15 minutes

Chinese Hot and Sour Soup

¼ pound boneless Pork Loin, cut into fine julienne strips
1 teaspoon Peanut Oil
1 teaspoon Corn Starch
½ teaspoon ground White Pepper
½ teaspoon ground Black Pepper

❖

4 large dried Shitake Mushrooms
8 cups Chicken Broth
½ cup thinly sliced fresh Mushrooms
½ cup thinly sliced Bamboo Shoots
½ cup finely chopped Water Chestnuts
2 tablespoons Soy Sauce
2 tablespoons Rice Wine
8 ounces Bean Curd (firm tofu)
2 large Whole Eggs, beaten
2 tablespoons Cornstarch
2 tablespoons Cold Water

❖

1 tablespoon Sesame Oil
¼ cup Rice Vinegar
3 tablespoons chopped Green Onion

Combine the first 5 ingredients in a small bowl. Set aside to marinate. Place the shitake mushrooms in a medium bowl and pour boiling water over them. Let stand for 15-20 minutes, or until soft. Drain and slice into ¼" strips (removing stems) and set aside. In a large stock pot, combine the chicken broth, marinated pork, shitake mushrooms, fresh mushrooms, bamboo shoots, water chestnuts, soy sauce, rice wine and bean curd. Bring to a boil over medium-high heat. Reduce the heat to a slow simmer. Pour the beaten eggs into the soup in a slow steady stream...stirring slowly. In a small bowl or cup, combine the 2 tablespoons of corn starch with the 2 tablespoons of cold water. When thoroughly mixed, pour into soup. Mix well and continue to simmer the soup. Just before serving, stir in the sesame oil, rice vinegar and chopped green onion. Serve immediately. Makes 2½-3 quarts.

Serving Size: 8 ounces   **Calories:** 119   **Total Fat:** 6.8 grams (52%)
Sat. Fat: 1.8 grams   **Cholesterol:** 45 mgs.
Sodium: 708 mgs.   **Carbohydrates:** 5.4 grams

Preparation time: 20-30 minutes   **Cooking Time:** 2 hours

Fresh Pea Soup

Unlike the more traditional Split Pea Soup, this soup features fresh (or frozen) green peas, as well as cabbage, potatoes and ham.

8 cups Chicken Broth
1 cup chopped fresh Onion
1 large smoked Ham Hock
2 Bay Leaves
¼ cup chopped fresh Basil
(or 1 tablespoon dried)
½ teaspoon freshly ground Black Pepper
½ teaspoon Salt
2 cups shredded Green Cabbage
3 cups fresh (or frozen) Green Peas
1 cup peeled and diced Potato

❖

1 tablespoon Sour Cream per serving for garnish

In a large stock pot over high heat, bring the chicken broth to a boil, while adding the onion, ham hock, bay leaves, basil pepper and salt. Reduce the heat and simmer, partially covered, for 1½ hours, or until the ham hock is very tender. Remove it from the broth, and set aside to cool. Meanwhile, add the cabbage, peas and potatoes and return the soup to a boil. Remove the meat from the hock and chop coarsely. Discard the fat and bones, and add the chopped meat to the soup. Reduce the heat and simmer the soup for an additional 30 minutes, uncovered. To serve, ladle into bowls, and top with a dollop of sour cream. Makes 3 quarts.

Serving Size: 8 ounces   **Calories:** 148   **Total Fat:** 7.1 grams (43%)
Sat. Fat: 3.2 grams   **Cholesterol:** 19 mgs.
Sodium: 690 mgs.   **Carbohydrates:** 11.4 grams

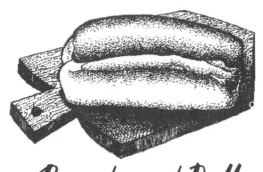

Breads and Rolls

Preparation Time: 15 minutes   **Rising Time:** 1-1¼ hours   **Baking Time:** 15-20 minutes

Foccacia con Aglio

Italian Garlic-Cheese Flat Bread

1 tablespoon Active Dry Yeast
1 teaspoon Sugar
1 cup warm Water (105°)
1 teaspoon Salt
2½-3 cups All Purpose Flour
2 teaspoons minced Garlic
2 tablespoons Extra Virgin Olive Oil
½ cup grated Parmesan Cheese
1 tablespoon Coarse Salt (or to taste)

In a large bowl, dissolve the yeast and sugar in the warm water. Let stand until bubbly...about 5 minutes. Stir in the salt and 2½ cups of the flour and stir just until moistened. Turn out onto a clean, dry counter-top and knead until smooth and elastic (about 10 minutes), adding additional flour as need to keep the dough from sticking. Place in an warm, oiled crockery bowl and turn to coat the top. Cover with a clean, dry towel, and let rise until doubled...about 1 hour. Meanwhile, heat the olive oil in a small skillet over medium heat, and sauté the garlic for 1 minute. Set aside to cool. When doubled, punch down the dough and knead lightly. Roll the dough out to fit into an oiled 10" X 15" rectangular jelly roll pan. With your index finger, pierce the dough at 1" intervals. Drizzle the garlic oil over the dough and spread it evenly over the top with your hands. Sprinkle with the Parmesan and salt, and let rise about 20 minutes in a warm place away from drafts. Bake 15-20 minutes at 400°, or until golden brown. Cut into 12 squares.

Serving Size: 1 square   **Calories:** 158   **Total Fat:** 3.8 grams (22%)
Sat. Fat: 1.2 grams   **Cholesterol:** 3.3 mgs.
Sodium: 656 mgs.   **Carbohydrates:** 25.1 grams

Preparation Time: 30-40 minutes   **Rising Time:** 3½ hours   **Baking Time:** 30-35 minutes

Beer Rye Bread

2 tablespoons Active Dry Yeast (2 packages)
½ cup Warm Water (105°)
½ cup Molasses, slightly warmed
12 ounces Dark Beer or Ale, at room temperature
4 tablespoons, melted Butter
2 teaspoons Salt
3 cups Rye Flour
3½-4 cups All Purpose White Flour
1 tablespoon Caraway Seed
1 Egg White, lightly beaten
1 tablespoon Poppy Seed or Coarse Salt

Combine the yeast and warm water, mixing well. Set aside for 5 minutes, or until bubbly. Combine the molasses and beer with the yeast mixture. Add the melted butter, salt, rye flour, and 2 cups of the white flour. Mix until stiff. Add 1½ cups more white flour and mix lightly with your hands. Turn the dough out onto a clean dry countertop and knead for 10-15 minutes, or until smooth and elastic, adding extra flour as needed to keep the dough from sticking. Place the dough in a warm, buttered bowl. Cover with a clean, dry towel, and let rise in a warm, draft-free place until doubled in bulk (about 1½-2 hours). Turn the dough out onto a floured surface and knead lightly. Shape into 2 loaves, and either place in buttered 4" X 8" bread pans, or on buttered baking sheets for a "free-form" loaf. Cover with a clean towel, and again let rise until doubled...about another hour and a half. Very gently, brush the top of the loaves with the beaten egg white and sprinkle with either poppy seeds or coarse salt. Bake in a preheated 375° oven for 35-45 minutes, or until done. Makes 2 loaves.

Serving Size: 1 slice (1/16 of loaf) **Calories:** 130   **Total Fat:** 2 grams (14%)
Sat. Fat: 1 gram   **Cholesterol:** 3.9 mgs.
Sodium: 153 mgs.   **Carbohydrates:** 24.5 grams

Preparation Time: 30 minutes   **Rising Time:** 1½ hours   **Baking Time:** 40 minutes

Hi-Rise Honey Whole Wheat Bread

2 cups Whole Wheat Flour
5-5½ cups All Purpose White Flour
2 tablespoons Active Dry Yeast
1 teaspoon Salt
¼ cup Olive Oil
¼ cup Honey
3 cups Hot Water (115°)

❖

2 tablespoons melted Butter

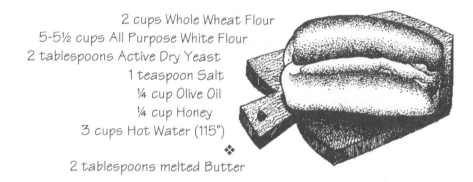

Combine the whole wheat flour, 2½ cups of the white flour, the yeast, salt, olive oil and honey in a large bowl, mixing well. Add the water all at once and beat with electric mixer for 3-4 minutes to develop the gluten in the flour. Add 1½-2 more cups of flour and turn the dough out onto a well floured countertop and knead until smooth and elastic (about 10 minutes), adding enough additional flour to keep the dough from sticking. Place the dough in a warm, oiled crockery bowl, turning once to coat the top. Cover with a clean, dry cloth and put in a warm, draft-free location to rise until doubled in size (about 40-45 minutes). Punch the dough down and knead lightly, then shape into 2 loaves. Place the loaves in 9" X 5" bread pans. Cover with a towel again, and let rise until doubled...about 40-45 minutes. Bake in a preheated 375° oven for 35-40 minutes, or until loaves are dark, golden brown. Remove the loaves from the oven and brush the tops with the melted butter. Place the pans on a rack to cool. Makes 2 loaves.

Serving Size: 1 slice (1/16 of loaf)   **Calories:** 132   **Total Fat:** 2.4 grams (16%)
Sat. Fat: Less than 1 gram   **Cholesterol:** 1 mg.
Sodium: 72 mgs.   **Carbohydrates:** 24.3 grams

JUST A NOTE: There's no such thing as a "bad" loaf of homemade bread...although certainly some are better than others. Try it! If you've never made bread before, you're going to love it! While it will take several hours to come up with the finished loaf...the actual amount of time you'll spend working the dough is minimal...and very satisfying.

Savory Sausage Bread

1 pound Sweet Italian Sausage
3 tablespoons Active Dry Yeast
7 cups All Purpose White Flour
1 tablespoon Sugar
1 teaspoon Salt
1 teaspoon EACH dried Basil and Oregano
1½ cups Whole Milk
¾ cup Water
2 tablespoons reserved Sausage Drippings
1 Whole Large Egg

❖

2 tablespoons Coarse Corn Meal
1 Egg White, lightly beaten
1 tablespoon Poppy Seeds

Remove the sausage from the casings. In a large skillet over medium-high heat, fry the sausage (crumble as it cooks) until nicely browned. Drain the sausage in a sieve, reserving 2 tablespoons of the drippings. Set aside. Combine the yeast, 3 cups of the flour, the sugar, salt and herbs in a large mixing bowl. Set aside. Combine the milk and water in a small saucepan, and heat on low to 130°. Combine the sausage drippings, egg, and the milk mixture with the flour/yeast mixture, stirring well. With an electric mixer, beat the batter on high speed for 1 minute. By hand, stir in the crumbled sausage. Add the remaining flour and mix lightly with your hands. Turn the dough out onto a clean, dry, floured countertop and knead for 10 minutes, or until smooth and elastic. Place the dough in a warmed and oiled bowl, turning to coat the top. Cover with a clean, dry towel, and let rise in a warm, draft-free spot until it doubles in size (about 1 hour). Punch down the dough and knead a minute or two more, then shape into 2 loaves. Place the loaves on greased baking sheet sprinkled with the corn meal, and cover with a towel. Let rise until doubled again...about 1 hour. Preheat oven to 375°. Lightly brush the tops of the loaves with the beaten egg white, and sprinkle them with the poppy seeds. With a sharp knife, slash the tops in a checkerboard pattern (about 1½" wide). Bake for 35-40 minutes, or until dark, golden brown. Makes 2 loaves.

Serving Size: 1 slice (1/16 of loaf)   **Calories:** 159   **Total Fat:** 4.6 grams (26%)
Sat. Fat: 1.7 grams   **Cholesterol:** 17 mgs.
Sodium: 247 mgs.   **Carbohydrates:** 22.8 grams

Preparation Time: 1 hour   **Rising & Fermenting Time:** Overnight + 2½ hours   **Baking Time:** 35-40 minutes

Crusty French Baguettes

This classic bread takes a little longer than most, because it requires
an overnight "sponge"...but the results are well worth it!

2 tablespoons Active Dry Yeast
2½ cups Warm Water (105°)
6-7 cups Bread Flour
2 teaspoons Salt

❖

2 tablespoons Corn Meal
1 tablespoon Cold Water
1 Egg White lightly beaten, with 1 tablespoon Cold Water

Combine the yeast and the warm water in a large bowl, mixing well. Set aside for 5 minutes, or until
bubbly. Add 2 cups of the flour, blending well. Cover with plastic wrap, and place in a warm place
(70-80°) for 8 hours or overnight. (The longer this "sponge" is allowed to ferment, the better it will
flavor the bread.) The next morning, add 4½ cups of the flour and the salt to the sponge, mixing well
until very stiff. Turn the dough out onto a clean, dry countertop and knead 15-20 minutes, adding
additional flour as needed to prevent it from sticking. Dust the ball of dough with flour and place it in a
warm bowl. Cover the bowl with a clean, damp towel and let rise in a warm, draft free place until 2-3
times its original size (about 1½ hours). Punch the dough down and knead lightly. Let rest for 5
minutes. Meanwhile, prepare the baking pans, by greasing them well, and sprinkling them with the
cornmeal. Then, shape the dough into 4 long, thin loaves (about 17" to 18" long) with slightly tapered
ends. Place them on the baking sheets. Cover with a clean, dry towel, and let rise until doubled (about 1
hour). Remove the oven racks, and place a 9" X 13" roasting pan in the bottom of the oven. Fill the pan
about half full with hot water. Position the oven racks in the lower part of the oven, and preheat to
425°. Make diagonal slashes in the tops of the loaves with a sharp knife. Brush the tops of the loaves
with cold water, and bake for 15 minutes. Brush the loaves with the beaten egg white and water glaze,
and bake 10 minutes more. Brush the loaves with the egg white glaze again, remove the roasting pan
with the water, and bake 10 minutes longer, or until the bread is a deep golden color, and sounds hollow
when tapped. Remove the loaves from the baking sheets and place them directly on the oven rack. Bake
for an additional 3-5 minutes to give the bread an extra crisp crust. Cool on racks. Makes 4 loaves.

Serving Size: 1 slice (1/8 of loaf)   **Calories:** 95.3   **Total Fat:** Less than 1 gram (3%)
Sat. Fat: Less than 1 gram   **Cholesterol:** 0 mgs.
Sodium: 136 mgs.   **Carbohydrates:** 19.8 grams

Toasted Pecan Bread

2 tablespoons Active Dry Yeast
1 cup Warm Water (105°)
2 tablespoons Honey
1½ cups All Purpose White Flour
1½ cups Whole Wheat Flour
½ teaspoon Salt
2 tablespoons melted Butter
1/3 cup chopped Pecans

❖

1 tablespoon Corn Meal
1 tablespoon Whipping Cream

In a medium bowl, combine the yeast, water and honey. Mix well and set aside for 5 minutes, or until bubbly. In a large mixing bowl, combine the flours, salt and melted butter. Then add the yeast mixture and mix well. Turn the dough out onto a clean, dry, floured countertop and begin to knead, adding more white flour as needed to keep the dough from sticking. Knead for 10 minutes, or until smooth and elastic. Place the dough in a large, warm, buttered bowl, turning to coat the top. Cover with a clean towel and place in a warm, draft free location to rise until doubled (about 45 minutes). Meanwhile, preheat the oven to 350°. Chop the pecans and scatter them on a baking sheet, and toast them in the center of the oven for 5-6 minutes. When the dough has risen, punch it down, and turn it out onto the countertop. Add the pecans, and knead them into the dough. Shape the dough into a nice round, and place it on a greased baking sheet sprinkled with the corn meal. Cover with a towel again, and let rise for 45 minutes (or until doubled). Just before baking, brush the loaf with the cream, and carefully slash a big X in the top (about ¼" deep) with a sharp knife. Bake at 350° for 30 to 35 minutes, or until the loaf sounds hollow when tapped. Makes 1 loaf.

Serving Size: 1 slice (1/16 of loaf)   **Calories:** 124   **Total Fat:** 3.7 grams (26%)
Sat. Fat: 1.2 grams   **Cholesterol:** 4.5 mgs.
Sodium: 83.4 mgs.   **Carbohydrates:** 20.5 grams

Oh, Nuts!
Actually, you can use most any type of nuts you have on hand for this recipe. Walnuts work very well...as would pistachios or even shelled sunflower seeds. Just make sure they are finely chopped...about the size of whole sunflower seeds...lightly toast them and proceed as usual.

Mediterranean Olive Bread

¾ cup finely chopped Onion
2 tablespoons Olive Oil
¾ cup chopped Black Olives
3½ cups All Purpose White Flour
2 tablespoons Active Dry Yeast
1 teaspoon Salt
2 teaspoons Sugar
1 cup Hot Water (115°)

❖

1 tablespoon Corn Meal

In a small skillet over medium heat, sauté the onion in the olive oil until it begins to turn a light golden brown. Remove the skillet from the heat, and stir in the olives. Set aside to cool slightly. Meanwhile, combine all the dry ingredients in a large bowl, mixing thoroughly. Add the water and mix with a large spoon, until mixing becomes difficult. Then, turn the dough out onto a floured countertop. Make a well in the center and add the olive-onion mixture, incorporating it into the dough. Knead until smooth and elastic (about 10 minutes), adding additional flour as needed to keep the dough from sticking. (Finished dough should be very stiff.) Place the dough in a warm, oiled crockery bowl, turning once to coat the top. Cover with a clean, dry towel, and place the bowl in a warm, draft-free location to rise until doubled...about 45 minutes. Punch down the dough and knead it lightly. Then, shape the dough into a round loaf, and place it on a greased baking sheet sprinkled with corn meal. Cover with the towel again, and let rise an additional 40-45 minutes until doubled. Bake in a 375° oven for 35-40 minutes, or until a deep, golden brown. NOTE: For a crispier crust, lower the baking temperature to 350°...brush the top periodically with cold water...and bake 5-10 minutes longer. Makes one large loaf.

Serving Size: 1 slice (1/16 of loaf)   **Calories:** 129   **Total Fat:** 2.7 grams (19%)
Sat. Fat: Less than 1 gram   **Cholesterol:** 0 mgs.
Sodium: 176 mgs.   **Carbohydrates:** 22.8 grams

About the crust...

Water, when brushed on a loaf before or during baking, gives bread a crispy crust. On the other hand, beaten whole egg mixed with a little water, gives the crust a shiny glaze, and helps hold toppings, like poppyseed, in place. Egg white, will also hold toppings, but tends to produce a chewier crust, as will a mixture of corn starch and water...while milk or melted butter yields a soft, tender crust.

Pepperoni-Onion Bread

1½ cups chopped Onion
3 tablespoons Butter
3 tablespoons Active Dry Yeast
½ cup Warm Water (105°)
1½ cups Whole Milk (at room temperature)
1 large Whole Egg (at room temperature)
2 tablespoons Sugar
1 teaspoon Salt
1 teaspoon dried Oregano Leaves
5½-6 cups All Purpose White Flour
3½-ounces Pepperoni Sausage, minced

❖

1 Egg White, lightly beaten
1 tablespoon Poppy Seeds

In a large skillet over medium heat, sauté the onion in the butter, until the onion is a rich, golden color. Set aside to cool. In a medium-size bowl, combine the yeast and warm water (mix well) and set aside for 5-10 minutes, or until bubbly. Meanwhile, combine the milk, egg, sugar, salt and oregano in a blender. Blend on medium for 30 seconds. In a large mixing bowl, combine the egg mixture, the sautéed onions, the minced pepperoni, yeast mixture and 4 cups of the flour. Mix well. Sprinkle 1 cup of flour over the dough and turn it out onto a well floured, dry countertop and knead thoroughly. Add extra flour as needed to keep the dough from sticking. Knead until smooth and elastic...about 10 minutes. Place bread dough in a large, oiled bowl, turning once to coat the top. Cover with a clean, dry towel, and place in a warm, draft-free spot. Let rise until doubled in bulk (about 1 hour). Punch down the dough and turn it out onto a floured countertop. Knead the dough briefly and shape it into two loaves. Place the loaves in 2 well greased 5" X 9" bread pans. Cover and let rise again, until doubled in size (about 1 hour). Very gently, brush the tops of the loaves with the beaten egg white and sprinkle with poppyseeds. Bake in a preheated 375° oven until a deep golden brown (about 35-40 minutes). Remove the bread from the oven and place the pans on a rack to cool for 10 minutes. Then remove the loaves from the pans and continue to cool. Enjoy at least some of the bread while it's still warm...then freeze or refrigerate the rest. Makes 2 loaves.

Serving Size: 1 slice (1/16th of loaf) **Calories:** 130 **Total Fat:** 3.4 grams (24%)
Sat. Fat: 1.5 grams **Cholesterol:** 13.5 mgs.
Sodium: 151 mgs. **Carbohydrates:** 20.3 grams

Grand Marnier Bread

Try it toasted, with Grand Marnier Butter!

2 tablespoons Active Dry Yeast
8-8½ cups All Purpose White Flour
2 teaspoons Salt
¼ cup Sugar
2 tablespoons Honey
2 large Whole Eggs
¼ cup Melted Butter
2 tablespoons grated Orange Zest
½ cup frozen Orange Juice Concentrate, at room temperature
2 tablespoons Grand Marnier Liqueur
2 cups Hot Water (115°)
½ cup Orange Marmalade

❖

1 Egg White beaten with 2 teaspoons Water for glaze

Combine the yeast, 5 cups of the flour, the salt, sugar, honey, eggs, melted butter, orange zest, orange juice concentrate and Grand Marnier in a large mixing bowl. Mix lightly. Add the hot water all at once, stirring well to combine. Beat with an electric mixer for 2-3 minutes. Add 3 more cups of flour and lightly work it in by hand. Turn the dough out onto a clean, dry, countertop and knead for 10 minutes, or until smooth and elastic, adding enough additional flour to keep the dough from sticking. Place the dough in a warm, buttered bowl, turning to coat all sides. Cover with a clean, dry towel, and let rise in a warm, draft free location until doubled (about 1½ hours). Punch the dough down, and knead lightly. Melt the marmalade in a small saucepan over low heat. Set aside to cool slightly. Divide the dough into 2 equal portions. Roll out each portion to a 9" X 12" rectangle. Using a pastry brush, spread ¼ cup of the marmalade on each portion, and roll up jelly roll style, starting with the 9" side. Place the loaves in buttered 5" X 9" bread pans. Cover with towels, and let rise in a warm place until they double again (about 1½ hours). Preheat oven to 375°. Gently brush the tops of the loaves with the egg white glaze and bake the loaves for 30-35 minutes, or until they are a deep golden brown on top, and sound hollow when tapped. Cool in the pans for 10 minutes. Then remove the loaves from the pans and let cool completely on a rack. Makes 2 loaves.

Serving Size: 1 slice (1/16 of loaf)   **Calories:** 158   **Total Fat:** 1.4 grams (8%)
Sat. Fat: Less than 1 gram   **Cholesterol:** 15.2 mgs.
Sodium: 149 mgs.   **Carbohydrates:** 31.8 grams

Bolillos

Mexican-style "French" rolls

2 tablespoons Active Dry Yeast
2 tablespoons Sugar
2 cups Warm Water (105°)
5-5½ cups Bread Flour
2 teaspoons Salt
2 tablespoons Olive Oil

❖

1 teaspoon Corn Starch dissolved in ½ cup water

In a large mixing bowl, combine the yeast, sugar and warm water. Stir well, and set aside for 5-7 minutes, or until yeast is bubbly. Add 3 cups of the flour, the salt and olive oil, mixing well with an electric mixer. Add 2 more cups of flour, blending slightly with your hands...then turn the dough out onto a clean, dry, floured countertop. Knead the dough for 10 minutes (or until smooth and elastic), adding additional flour as needed to keep the dough from sticking. Place the dough in a warm, oiled crockery bowl...turning to coat all sides. Cover with a clean, damp cloth, and place is a warm, draft free spot to rise until doubled (about 35-40). Punch the dough down and turn it out onto a clean countertop. Knead lightly, then let rest for 5 minutes. Divide the dough into 24 equal portions and shape each portion into an egg shape...then pinch and pull the ends to make sharp points. Place the rolls on greased baking sheets...12 to a sheet. Cover the rolls with clean, dry towels, and let them rise for 35-40 minutes, or until doubled. In a small saucepan, bring the cornstarch/water mixture to a boil over medium heat, stirring constantly. Set aside and let cool. Just before baking, brush the rolls lightly with the mixture. Bake in a preheated 375° oven for 25-30 minutes, or until the rolls are golden brown. Half way through the baking, rotate the trays and switch the top tray with the bottom tray, so that the rolls can bake evenly. Let cool on racks. Best if served warm...but can be reheated for 5-7 minutes in a 350° oven. Makes 24 rolls.

Serving Size: 1 roll **Calories:** 120 **Total Fat:** 1.4 grams (11%)
Sat. Fat: Less than 1 gram **Cholesterol:** 0 mgs.
Sodium: 179 mgs. **Carbohydrates:** 23.1 grams

Cheesy Onion Twist

For the Bread:
1 tablespoon Active Dry Yeast
¼ cup Warm Water (105°)
4 cups All Purpose White Flour
¼ cup Sugar
1½ teaspoons Salt
½ cup Hot Water (115°)
½ cup Whole Milk
4 tablespoons softened Butter
1 Whole Egg, lightly beaten

❖

For the Filling:
4 tablespoons Butter
1 cup minced fresh Onion
2 tablespoons grated Parmesan Cheese
1 tablespoon Poppy Seed
¼ teaspoon Granulated Garlic (or Garlic Powder)
¾ teaspoon Salt
1 teaspoon Paprika

In a large bowl, dissolve the yeast in the warm water. Set aside for 5 minutes, or until bubbly. Then add 2 cups of the flour and the remaining bread ingredients in the order given. With an electric mixer on low speed, blend until thoroughly mixed. By hand, stir in the remaining flour to form a soft dough. Knead for 10 minutes, or until smooth and elastic, adding more flour as needed to keep the dough from sticking. Place in a warm, oiled crockery bowl, turning to coat the top. Cover and let the dough rise until doubled in bulk...about 1 hour. Meanwhile, prepare the filling, by melting the butter in a small skillet over medium heat. Add the remaining filling ingredients, mixing well. Set aside. When the dough is doubled in size, punch it down and place it on a floured countertop. Knead lightly. Let rest 5 minutes. Roll out the dough into a 12" X 18" rectangle. Spread the filling evenly onto the dough. Cut the dough lengthwise into three 4" X 18" strips, beginning with the 18" side, so that you have three, long "ropes". Transfer the ropes to a buttered cookie sheet and braid together. Cover with a clean, dry towel and let rise until doubled again...about 1 hour. Bake in a pre-heated 350° oven for 45 minutes, or until deep golden brown. Makes 1 large loaf.

Serving Size: 1 slice (1/16 of loaf) **Calories:** 198 **Total Fat:** 7 grams (33%)
Sat. Fat: 4 grams **Cholesterol:** 30 mgs.
Sodium: 382 mgs. **Carbohydrates:** 28.7 grams

Preparation Time: 30 minutes   **Rising Time:** 2 hours   **Baking Time:** 40-45 minutes

English Milk Loaf

2 tablespoons Active Dry Yeast
2 teaspoons Sugar
1 cup Whole Milk, warmed to 105°
4½-5 cups Bread Flour
1 teaspoon Salt
¼ cup Butter, melted
1 large Whole Egg, lightly beaten

Combine the yeast, sugar and warm milk in a large bowl, stirring well. Set aside for 5 minutes, or until bubbly. Add 2 cups of the flour, the salt, melted butter and beaten egg and mix well with an electric mixer. Add 2 more cups of flour and mix lightly with your hands. Scrape the dough out onto a clean, dry, floured countertop and begin to knead. Knead until smooth and elastic (about 10 minutes), adding extra flour as needed to keep the dough from sticking. Place the dough in a buttered, warm bowl, turning to coat all sides. Cover with a clean, damp towel, and place the bowl in a warm location to rise until doubled (about 1 hour). Punch the dough down and knead lightly. Divide in half, and shape each portion into two loaves. Place in buttered 9" X 5" bread pans. Cover and let rise until doubled again...about 1 hour. Gently brush the loaves with milk, and bake in a preheated 375° oven for 40-45 minutes, or until loaves shrink from the sides, and the top is dark golden brown. Cool on a wire rack. Makes 2 loaves.

Serving Size: 1 slice (1/16 of loaf)   **Calories:** 86.1   **Total Fat:** 2.0 grams (22%)
Sat. Fat: 1.1 grams   **Cholesterol:** 11.5 mgs.
Sodium: 87.5 mgs.   **Carbohydrates:** 14.2 grams

♥
A Word or Two About Bread Machines...
Everyone asks me what I think about bread machines, and I suppose my answer is a little biased. If the convenience of making bread with an automated machine is enough to tempt you into making bread...then by all means, use a bread machine. If you are familiar with your particular brand of machine, you can easily adapt most of these recipes for that purpose. But in my opinion, you're missing the real joy of breadmaking...kneading a loaf with your own hands, and watching it turn into a flavorful and nutritious "gift" that you can give your family. And, I have never tasted a loaf of machine-made bread that could hold a candle to the texture and overall appearance obtained with hand kneading. So save yourself a lot of money...use the best "bread machine" anyone ever invented...your own two hands!

Herb Pretzels

2 tablespoons Active Dry Yeast
1 tablespoon Sugar
¾ cup Warm Water (105°)
4½-5 cups Bread Flour
1 teaspoon EACH Oregano, Basil and Thyme
¼ teaspoon freshly ground Black Pepper
2 teaspoons Salt
¼ cup Extra Virgin Olive Oil
¾ cup Buttermilk, at room temperature

❖

1 Egg White, lightly beaten
1-2 tablespoons Coarse Salt

In a small bowl, combine the yeast, sugar and warm water. Set aside for 5 minutes, or until bubbly. In a large bowl, combine 2½ cups of the flour, the herbs, pepper and salt. Mix well. Add the olive oil, buttermilk and yeast mixture, and beat with an electric mixer for 2-3 minutes. Add 2 cups additional flour and mix lightly with your hands. Then, turn the dough out onto a clean, dry, countertop and begin kneading. Add extra flour as needed to keep the dough from sticking. Knead for 10-12 minutes, or until smooth and elastic. Place the dough in a warm, oiled bowl, turning to coat all sides. Cover with a dry towel, and place in a warm, draft free location to rise until doubled (about 1 hour). Punch the dough down and turn it out onto a countertop and knead lightly. Let rest for 5 minutes. Meanwhile, butter 2 large baking sheets and preheat the oven to 400°. Divide the dough into 4 equal portions. Then, divide each of those into 6 equal portions. Roll each portion into a long rope about the size of your little finger, and 12"-14" long. Twist each portion into a pretzel shape, and place them on the baking sheets (12 per sheet) and cover them lightly with a towel. Let them rise in a warm place until doubled (about 45 minutes.) Just before baking, brush the pretzels with the beaten egg white, and sprinkle them with the coarse salt. Bake for 15-20 minutes, or until lightly browned. Serve hot. Makes 2 dozen rolls.

Serving Size: 1 twist   **Calories:** 113   **Total Fat:** 2.6 grams (21%)
Sat. Fat: Less than 1 gram   **Cholesterol:** Less than 1 mg.
Sodium: 455 mgs.   **Carbohydrates:** 19.1 grams

Scottish Baps

A sturdy and flavorful roll to serve for breakfast, or to accompany a hot bowl of soup.
This is an adaptation of an authentic Scottish recipe from the turn of the century.

2/3 cup Warm Water (105°)
2/3 cup Warm Whole Milk (105°)
1 tablespoon Active Dry Yeast
3¼ cups Bread Flour
2 teaspoons Salt

❖

2 tablespoons Milk
Extra Flour for dusting the Baps before baking

Fill a large crockery bowl with hot water. Let it stand for 5 minutes. Meanwhile, combine the water, milk and yeast in a medium bowl. Mix well and set aside for 5-10 minutes. Empty the bowl, and dry it thoroughly. Sift 3 cups of the flour and the salt into the bowl. Add the yeast/milk mixture all at once. Mix lightly. Using your hands, lightly knead the dough in the bowl...just enough to incorporate the flour. Cover the bowl with a clean, dry towel, and put it in a warm, draft free place until the dough has doubled...about 1 hour. Punch the dough down and sprinkle the remaining flour over the top of the dough. Mix lightly with your hands...then scrape the dough out onto a clean, dry countertop. Knead the dough for 3-4 minutes...adding a little extra, if needed, to keep it from sticking. The dough should be very soft. Divide it into 8 equal pieces, and with your hands, shape each portion into an oval roll about 3" wide X 4" long X ½" thick. Flour the rolls as you shape them, and place them on a greased and floured baking sheet. Cover with a clean, dry towel, and let rise again for 30 minutes, or until light and puffed. Preheat oven to 425°. Just before baking, brush the tops and sides with milk, and dust with more flour. With your index finger, make a deep indentation in the center of each bap. Bake for 15-20 minutes, or until light golden in color. Remove to a wire rack. Serve warm, right from the oven. Makes 8 rolls.

Serving Size: 1 bap   **Calories:** 245   **Total Fat:** 1.5 grams (5%)
Sat. Fat: Less than 1 gram   **Cholesterol:** 3.3 mgs.
Sodium: 547 mgs.   **Carbohydrates:** 49.2 grams

Whole Wheat English Muffins

3 tablespoons Active Dry Yeast
1 teaspoon Sugar
1 cup Warm Water (105°)
1 cup Whole Wheat Flour
¼ cup Toasted Wheat Germ
1½ teaspoons Salt
4½-5 cups Bread Flour
1 cup Whole Milk, at room temperature
¼ cup Honey
¼ cup (½ stick) Butter, melted

❖

3 tablespoons coarse Corn Meal

In a medium mixing bowl, combine the yeast, sugar and warm water, mixing well. Set aside for 5 minutes, or until bubbly. In a large bowl, combine the whole wheat flour, wheat germ, salt, and 3 cups of the bread flour. Mix well. To the dry ingredients, add the milk, honey, melted butter and yeast mixture, blending well with an electric mixer. Add another cup of the flour, and mix lightly with your hands. Turn the dough out onto a clean, dry, floured countertop. Knead until smooth and elastic (about 15 minutes), adding more flour as needed to keep the dough from sticking. Let the dough rest for 5 minutes. Roll the dough out on a floured countertop to a thickness of ½". Cut with a cookie cutter into 3" rounds. Place the rounds on a baking sheet sprinkled with the corn meal. Gather up any scraps and re-roll to ½" and cut more rounds, using all the dough. Cover the muffins with a clean, dry towel, and let rise until doubled (about 30 minutes). Heat a griddle for 5-6 minutes on medium heat. Place the muffins on the griddle and bake for 2-3 minutes per side, or until the top springs back to the touch. Let cool on a wire rack. To serve, split horizontally with a fork. Toast and serve hot with butter. Makes 24 muffins.

Serving Size: 1 muffin   **Calories:** 148   **Total Fat:** 2.8 grams (17%)
Sat. Fat: 1.5 grams   **Cholesterol:** 6.6 mgs.
Sodium: 159 mgs.   **Carbohydrates:** 26.9 grams

For Faster Rising Dough...

...run hot water in a heavy crockery bowl and let it stand for 2-3 minutes. Then empty the bowl and dry it thoroughly. Oil or butter the bowl before placing the dough in it to keep it from sticking. And, turn it over to coat the top, as well. Cover the bowl with a clean towel and step back! This will "jump start" the rising process, and yield a very nice loaf.

Chile-Cheese Cornbread

1 cup Yellow Cornmeal
1 cup All Purpose White Flour
1 tablespoon Baking Powder
½ teaspoon Salt
¼ cup Vegetable Oil
1 large Whole Egg, lightly beaten
1 cup Milk
¼ cup minced fresh Onion
¼ cup canned chopped Pimento
½ tablespoon minced fresh Serrano or Jalapeño Chili
½ cup shredded Extra Sharp Cheddar Cheese
½ cup frozen Corn, defrosted under hot running water
¼ cup sliced Ripe Olives

In a large bowl, combine the cornmeal, flour, baking powder and salt. Set aside. In another bowl, mix the oil, egg, milk, onion, pimento, chili, cheddar and corn. Fold the liquid ingredients into the dry ingredients, just until blended. Do not over mix. Spread batter evenly in a greased and floured 8" square baking pan. Sprinkle the sliced olives over the top. Bake in a preheated 400° oven for 30-35 minutes, or until a toothpick, when inserted in the center, comes out clean. Let cool 5 minutes, then cut into squares and serve warm. Makes 9 servings.

Serving Size: 1 square   **Calories:** 226   **Total Fat:** 10.4 grams (41%)
Sat. Fat: 2.6 grams   **Cholesterol:** 33.9 mgs.
Sodium: 301 mgs.   **Carbohydrates:** 27 grams

Mile High Popovers

Light and crispy on the outside...moist and hollow on the inside!
This is a very traditional popover recipe...but with some tips that will show you
how to make the lightest, highest popovers you've ever eaten!

2 Extra Large Whole Eggs
1 cup of Whole Milk
1 cup All Purpose White Flour
1 teaspoon Salt
2 tablespoons Butter, melted

With a wire whisk, beat the eggs thoroughly in a large bowl. Add the milk and continue to whisk until well
blended. Set aside. Sift the flour and salt together. Gradually add the flour mixture to the egg
mixture, whisking until well blended. Heavily butter a non-stick muffin or popover pan. Ladle the batter
into the prepared pan, filling to within ¼" of the top. Place in a COLD oven. Turn the oven on to 450°.
Now, go away and leave them alone for at least 25 minutes. (I KNOW...it's SO tempting to peek!) At
25-30 minutes, begin checking to see when they are done. The popovers should be a dark golden brown.
Remove them from the oven and serve immediately. Makes 10 popovers.

Serving Size: 1 popover   **Calories:** 95.6   **Total Fat:** 4.2 grams (40%)
Sat. Fat: 2.3 grams   **Cholesterol:** 51.9 mgs.
Sodium: 261 mgs.   **Carbohydrates:** 10.8 grams

Perfect Popover Tips

TIP #1: Have all ingredients at room temperature.
TIP #2: Do NOT preheat the oven.
TIP #3: Use a non-stick pan, making sure the non-stick coating is not marred.
TIP #4: Do NOT peek until the popovers have baked at least 25 minutes.
TIP #5: Be sure to bake until dark golden brown...under-baked popovers
will fall as soon as you take them from the oven.

Shredded Wheat Bread

There are many recipes for this flavorful wheat
bread...this is my personal adaptation.

3 large Shredded Wheat Biscuits, crumbled
½ cup Dark Molasses
¼ cup (½ stick) Butter, softened
1 teaspoon Salt
2 cups Whole Milk
2 tablespoons Active Dry Yeast
1 tablespoon Sugar
½ cup warm Water (105°)
¼ cup Wheat Germ
1 cup Whole Wheat Flour
4½-5 cups Bread Flour

❖

2 tablespoons melted Butter

In a large bowl, combine the crumbled shredded wheat biscuits, molasses, softened butter and salt. Set
aside. In a small saucepan over medium-high heat, bring the milk to a simmer, stirring occasionally.
Pour the hot milk over the shredded wheat mixture, and stir well. Set aside to cool. In a small bowl,
combine the yeast, sugar and warm water, stirring until dissolved. Let stand for 5 minutes, or until
bubbly. In a large bowl, combine the wheat germ, whole wheat flour, and 2 cups of the bread flour. Mix
the shredded wheat/milk mixture and the yeast mixture with the flours in the large bowl. Stir until all
the ingredients are moistened, then beat with an electric mixer for 2 minutes on medium speed. Add the
remaining flour and mix lightly with your hands. Turn the mixture out onto a clean, dry countertop and
knead for 15 minutes adding extra flour as needed to keep the dough from sticking. Place the dough ball
in a warm, buttered crockery bowl, turning to coat all sides. Cover with a clean, dry towel, and place in a
warm, draft free location to rise until doubled (about 1 hour). Punch the dough down and knead it lightly.
Let rest for five minutes. Meanwhile, butter two 9" X 5" loaf pans. Divide the dough into two equal
parts. Shape each half into a loaf, and place in the prepared pan. Cover the pans with a clean, dry
towel and set aside to rise until doubled again (about 1 hour). Gently brush the tops of the loaves with
the melted butter and bake them in a preheated 350° oven for 30-35 minutes, or until dark brown
on top, and the loaves sound hollow when tapped. Makes 2 loaves.

Serving Size: 1 slice (1/16 of loaf)   **Calories:** 127   **Total Fat:** 2.2 grams (15%)
Sat. Fat: 1.2 grams   **Cholesterol:** 4.8 mgs.
Sodium: 84.2 mgs.   **Carbohydrates:** 23.9 grams

Tomato-Parmesan Bow Knots

2 cups Whole Milk
¼ cup (½ stick) Butter
1 tablespoon Sugar
2 tablespoons Active Dry Yeast
5-5½ cups Bread Flour
1 teaspoon Salt
½ cup Sun Dried Tomatoes, finely chopped
1 cup grated Parmesan Cheese

❖

1 Whole Egg, lightly beaten

In a small saucepan, heat the milk until it just begins to simmer around the edges. Do not boil. Remove from heat, and add the butter. Stir until melted. Let cool to 105°. Sprinkle the sugar and yeast over the top, then stir until dissolved. Set aside for 5 minutes, or until bubbly. Combine 2 cups of the flour, the salt, sun dried tomatoes, cheese and yeast mixture. Mix well. Add 3 cups additional flour, and mix lightly with your hands. Turn the mixture out onto a clean, dry countertop, and knead for 10-12 minutes, adding extra flour as needed to keep the dough from sticking. Warm a large, crockery bowl in hot water. Dry thoroughly... then butter well. Place the dough in the bowl, turning to coat it on all sides. Cover with a clean, dry towel, and place in a warm, draft free location to rise until doubled...45 minutes. Punch the

dough down and knead lightly. Let the dough rest for 5 minutes, while you butter 2 large baking sheets. Divide the dough into 24 equal portions. Roll each portion into ropes about the size of your thumb, and 10-12 inches long. Tie each rope in a knot, and place it on the prepared baking sheet. Cover with a towel, and let rise until doubled again...about 45 minutes. Preheat oven to 375°. Brush with beaten egg and bake for 15-20 minutes, or until golden brown. Serve warm. Makes 24 bow knots.

Serving Size: 1 bow knot **Calories:** 162 **Total Fat:** 4.4 grams (25%)
Sat. Fat: 2.5 grams **Cholesterol:** 20.1 mgs.
Sodium: 223 mgs. **Carbohydrates:** 24.4 grams

❤
Sugar, Salt and Yeast
For yeast to become active, it must be mixed with warm liquid (water, milk, etc.) and "fed". Sugar provides the energy to make yeast more active. Recipes that call for sugar (or molasses, honey, etc.) to be mixed with the yeast will become "active" more quickly. Salt, on the other hand, slows the action of the yeast, and acts to stabilize it, yielding

Honey Oatmeal Bread

2 cups Rolled Oats (regular or quick cooking)
½ cup Honey
¼ cup (½ stick) Butter, softened
2 teaspoons Salt
1½ cups Boiling Water
2 tablespoons Active Dry Yeast
1 teaspoon Sugar
1 cup Warm Water (105°)
1 cup Whole Wheat Flour
3½-4 cups Bread Flour

❖

1 Egg White, lightly beaten with 1 tablespoon Water
6 tablespoons Rolled Oats

In a large bowl, combine the rolled oats, honey, butter (cut into pieces), salt and boiling water. Stir well, then set aside to cool. Next, combine the yeast, sugar and warm water in a small bowl, and stir to dissolve. Set aside for 5 minutes, or until bubbly. Then, add the whole wheat flour, 2 cups of the bread flour, and the yeast mixture to the honey/oat mixture, and stir until all the ingredients are moistened. Then add the remaining flour and mix lightly with your hands. Turn the mixture out onto a clean, dry countertop and knead for 15 minutes, or until smooth and elastic, adding extra bread flour as need to keep the dough from sticking. Place the dough in a warm, buttered crockery bowl and cover it with a clean, dry towel. Put in a warm, draft free place to rise until doubled (about 1 hour). Punch the dough down and knead it lightly. Let rest for 5 minutes. Meanwhile, generously grease two 5" X 9" bread pans. Place two tablespoons of the remaining oatmeal in each of the bread pans. (Reserve the other 2 tablespoons of oatmeal) To coat evenly, tilt the pan and tap it on the outside, turning the pan in several directions, until a fairly even coating is achieved. Divide the dough in half and shape each half into a loaf. Place the loaves in the prepared pans, and cover them with a clean, dry towel. Set aside to rise until doubled again (about 1 hour). Gently brush the loaves with the beaten egg white and water...then sprinkle them with the remaining rolled oats (1 tablespoon per loaf). Bake in a preheated 375° oven for 35-40 minutes, or until deep golden brown. Makes 2 loaves.

Serving Size: 1 slice (1/16 of loaf)   Calories: 124   Total Fat: 2.1 grams (15%)
Sat. Fat: 1 gram   Cholesterol: 3.9 mgs.
Sodium: 137 mgs.   Carbohydrates: 23.3 grams

Potato Rolls

A soft and comforting bread...a great accompaniment for a variety of soups.

2 tablespoons Active Dry Yeast
1 tablespoon Sugar
½ cup Warm Water (105°)
½ cup (1 stick) Butter, softened
1¼ cups hot Whole Milk (115°-120°)
1 cup Mashed Potatoes (prepared instant mashed potatoes are fine)
2 large Whole Eggs
2 teaspoons Salt
¼ cup Sugar
7-7½ cups Bread Flour

In a small bowl, combine the yeast, 1 tablespoon sugar and warm water, stirring to dissolve. Set aside. Meanwhile, combine the softened butter, hot milk, mashed potatoes, eggs, salt, ¼ cup sugar and 3 cups of the flour. Add the yeast mixture, and mix until all ingredients are moistened. Beat for 2 minutes on medium speed with an electric mixer. Then add the remaining flour and mix lightly with your hands. Turn the dough out onto a clean, dry countertop. Knead for 10-12 minutes, or until the dough is smooth and elastic, adding extra flour as needed to keep it from sticking. Place the dough in a warm, buttered crockery bowl and cover it with a clean, dry towel. Set in a warm, draft free location to rise until doubled (about 1 hour). Punch the dough down and knead it lightly. Then divide it into 24 equal portions. With your hands, shape each portion into a flat oval. Dip each roll in flour and place it on a baking sheet (12 rolls per baking sheet). Do not grease the baking sheet. Cover the rolls with clean, dry towels and let them rise in a warm place until doubled again...about 45 minutes. Bake in a preheated 400° oven until the rolls are lightly browned...about 15-20 minutes. Cool on wire racks. Makes 24 rolls.

Serving Size: 1 roll   **Calories:** 302   **Total Fat:** 5.5 grams (24%)
Sat. Fat: 3.1 grams   **Cholesterol:** 30.8 mgs.
Sodium: 255 mgs.   **Carbohydrates:** 32.7 grams

JUST A NOTE: If your loaf ends up with large holes in the center, you probably just needed to work out the bubbles in the dough before you shape it. That's why in most recipes I suggest a light kneading before shaping. It won't effect the flavor of the loaf...but it's a little hard to make sandwiches with slices of bread that look like Swiss cheese!

Preparation Time: 30 minutes   **Rising Time:** 2 hours   **Baking Time:** 30-35 minutes

Pane Parmigiano

Sun-dried Tomato and Cheese Bread

5½-6 cups Bread Flour
2 tablespoons Active Dry Yeast
1 tablespoon Sugar
1 teaspoon Salt
¼ cup Extra Virgin Olive Oil
½ cup chopped Sun-dried Tomatoes (packed in
oil) + 1 tablespoon of the oil (about 6 ounces total)
2 teaspoons minced fresh Garlic
2 cups Hot Water (110° to 115°)
1½ cups grated Parmesan Cheese

❖

1 Egg White, whisked with 1 tablespoon Water, for glaze
1-2 tablespoons Poppy Seeds

In a large bowl, combine 3 cups of the flour, the yeast, sugar, salt, olive oil, sun-dried tomatoes (with oil), garlic and hot water. Beat with an electric mixer for 1 minute. Add 2½ additional cups of flour and mix lightly with your hands. Turn the mixture out onto a clean, dry countertop. Knead for 10-12 minutes, or until smooth and elastic, adding enough additional flour to keep from sticking. Place the dough in a warm, oiled, crockery bowl, turning to coat all sides. Cover with a clean, dry towel, and let rise in a warm location until doubled (about 1 hour). Punch the dough down and knead briefly. Let rest for 5 minutes, then divide the dough into 2 equal portions. Roll out each portion to a 9" X 12" rectangle. Sprinkle with the grated cheese (¾ cup per loaf). Place the loaves in greased 9" X 5" bread pans and cover with towels. Let rise until doubled again...about 1 hour. Gently brush the tops with the egg white glaze and sprinkle with poppyseeds. Bake in a preheated 375° oven for 30-35 minutes, or until deep golden brown, and the bread begins to pull away from the sides of the pan.
Cool on racks. Makes 2 loaves.

Serving Size: 1 slice (1/16 of loaf)   **Calories:** 136   **Total Fat:** 4.1 grams (27%)
Sat. Fat: 1.2 grams   **Cholesterol:** 3.7 mgs.
Sodium: 169 mgs.   **Carbohydrates:** 19.9 grams

JUST A NOTE: The more shortening in a recipe, the softer the texture of the bread will be.

Irish Soda Bread

4 cups All Purpose White Flour
1 teaspoon Baking Soda
2 teaspoons Baking Powder
1 teaspoon Salt
2 tablespoons Sugar
2 teaspoons Caraway Seeds
¼ cup (½ stick) Butter
¾ cup dried Currants
1½ cups Buttermilk
¼ cup Irish Whiskey
1 tablespoon Butter, melted

Generously butter two 8" round cake pans. Set aside. In a large bowl, combine the flour, baking soda, baking powder, salt, sugar and caraway seeds. Using a pastry blender (or two knives), cut in the butter until the mixture resembles coarse meal. Gently stir in the currants. Mix the buttermilk and whiskey separately, then add them all at once to the flour mixture. Mix quickly and lightly...just enough to moisten the dry ingredients. Do not over mix! The secret to really good Irish Soda Bread is not to toughen the dough by over mixing. Turn out onto a floured countertop and knead together...no more than 30-60 seconds. (Dough will be sticky.) Divide the dough in half, and place it in the pans...pressing it evenly into the bottom. Brush the tops with the melted butter,

then slash deep crosses (½" deep) in the them. Place them in a warm, draft free location and let them "rest" for 30 minutes. Bake in a preheated 350° oven for 35-40 minutes, or until the loaves sound hollow when tapped. Cool on racks. To serve, slice thinly and serve warm from the oven...or try it toasted! Makes 2 loaves.

Serving Size: 1 slice (1/16 of loaf)   Calories: 95   Total Fat: 2.1 grams (20%)
Sat. Fat: 1.2 grams   Cholesterol: 5.3 mgs.
Sodium: 141 mgs.   Carbohydrates: 15.9 grams

❤

Cooling and Storing Bread

Breads should be cooled on a rack in a draft free location. When completely cool, wrap the bread in plastic wrap, and then place it in a zip-top plastic bag. It can then be stored in the refrigerator (If you plan to use it right away), or in the freezer for up to 3 months. If you are using frozen bread, simply thaw for an hour or so at room temperature and serve. If you are planning to serve dinner rolls, defrosting is not necessary...just warm them in a 350° oven for 10 minutes prior to serving.

Lavosh

Crisp Armenian Cracker Bread
Great for cheese and meat spreads...or plain with soup!

1 cup warm Water (105°)
1 tablespoon Active Dry Yeast
1 teaspoon Sugar
2 tablespoons Butter, melted
1 teaspoon Salt
2½-3 cups Bread Flour

Place the water in a large bowl, and sprinkle the yeast and sugar over the top. Stir to dissolve, and set aside for 5 minutes, or until bubbly. Then, add the melted butter, salt and 1 cup of the flour. With an electric mixer, beat for 2 minutes on medium speed. Add another cup or so of the flour and lightly mix it in with your hands. Turn the mixture out onto a clean, dry counter top and knead until smooth and elastic (about 10 minutes) adding extra flour as needed to keep from sticking. Place in a warm, buttered bowl and cover with a towel. Let rise until doubled (about ½ hour). Punch down the dough, and knead it lightly. Let rest for 5 minutes, then divide into 12 equal portions for large crackers...24 equal portions for small crackers. Place a large baking stone in a cold oven. Preheat the oven to 400°. Shape and bake only the number of rounds your baking stone can accommodate for each baking. (Mine is a large round one for pizza, and will hold 2 large, or 4 small rounds if you stagger the starting times). Cover the unbaked portions with a dry towel until baking time. Then, with a rolling pin, roll each ball of dough out to a round approximately 8" to 9" in diameter for large crackers...4" to 5" for small crackers... on a clean, well floured countertop. Prick the round in several places with a fork. Carefully place each round onto the baking stone. Bake for 5-7 minutes, or until golden brown, turning once for the last minute of baking. Cool on racks. Store in an airtight container.
Makes 12 large or 24 small cracker breads.

Serving Size: 1 round   **Calories:** 134   **Total Fat:** 2.3 grams (15%)
Sat. Fat: 1.2 grams   **Cholesterol:** 5.2 mgs.
Sodium: 199 mgs.   **Carbohydrates:** 24.4 grams

JUST A NOTE: Crush leftover lavosh and use it in meatballs or meatloaf...or feed it to your birds!

Spreads and Butters

Grand Marnier Butter

1 cup (2 sticks) Sweet Creamery (unsalted) Butter, at room temperature
¼ cup Honey
2 teaspoons grated Orange Peel
¼ cup Grand Marnier Liqueur

In a small bowl, combine the butter, honey and grated orange peel. With an electric mixer, beat the mixture on medium speed for 2 minutes. With the mixer running, gradually add the Grand Marnier. When the liqueur if completely incorporated, turn the mixer to high, and beat for another 2 minutes. Store in the refrigerator in an air-tight plastic container. Let stand at room temperature for 30 minutes before serving. Makes 1½ cups.

Serving Size: 1 teaspoon   **Calories:** 28   **Total Fat:** 2.6 grams (80%)
Sat. Fat: 1.5 grams   **Cholesterol:** 6.9 mgs.
Sodium: Less than 1 mg.   **Carbohydrates:** Less than 1 gram

Mexicali Cheese Spread

4 ounces Cream Cheese, at room temperature
3 ounces grated Extra Sharp Cheddar Cheese, at room temperature
1 tablespoon Chili Powder
1 teaspoon Onion Powder
½ teaspoon Garlic Powder
1 teaspoon dried Oregano
¼ teaspoon ground Cumin
1 tablespoon dried Cilantro
1 tablespoon Green Chili Salsa
1 teaspoon Worcestershire Sauce

Combine all the ingredients in the work bowl of a food processor fitted with a steel blade. Process for 60 seconds, or until smooth, scraping down the sides of the work bowl as needed. Store in an air-tight plastic container in the refrigerator. Let stand at room temperature for 30 minutes before serving.
Makes about 1 cup.

Serving Size: 1 tablespoon **Calories:** 49.2 **Total Fat:** 4.3 grams (77%)
Sat. Fat: 2.7 grams **Cholesterol:** 13.4 mgs.
Sodium: 66 mgs. **Carbohydrates:** Less than 1 gram

Hazelnut Butter

½ cup shelled Hazelnuts
1 cup (2 sticks) Sweet Creamery (unsalted) Butter, at room temperature
¼ cup Honey
¼ cup Franjelico Liqueur

Preheat oven to 350°. Spread the shelled hazelnuts in a single layer in a pie pan. Roast the hazelnuts in the oven for 15 minutes, stirring and checking periodically to make sure that they don't burn. The hazelnuts are done when the skins crack and begin to peel away from the nuts. Remove from the oven and let cool for 5 minutes. Place the nuts in a clean, dry terry towel, and rub briskly to remove the skins. All the skins will not come completely off the nuts, but do your best to remove most of the skins. Let cool completely. In a food processor fitted with a steel blade, pulse the nuts, until they are finely ground. Set aside. In a small bowl, blend the butter, honey and toasted hazelnuts with an electric mixer on medium speed for 2 minutes. With the mixer still running, gradually add the Franjelico. Continue mixing until the Franjelico is completely incorporated into the butter. Then, turn the mixer to high speed, and beat for an additional 2 minutes. Store in an air-tight plastic container in the refrigerator. Let stand at room temperature for 30 minutes before serving. Makes about 2 cups.

Serving Size: 1 teaspoon   **Calories:** 27.1   **Total Fat:** 2.5 grams (80%)
Sat. Fat: 1.3 grams   **Cholesterol:** 5.5 mgs.
Sodium: Less than 1 mg.   **Carbohydrates:** 1 gram

Preparation time: 10 minutes

Gorgonzola Spread

6 ounces Gorgonzola Cheese
3 ounces Cream Cheese
4 tablespoons (½ stick) Butter
Dash of Cayenne Pepper

Have all ingredients at room temperature. Place them in the work bowl of a food processor fitted with a steel blade. Pulse three or four times to begin mixing. Scrape down the sides of the work bowl. Then process for 1 minute, scraping down the sides again, as needed. Store in an air tight plastic container in the refrigerator until needed. Let stand at room temperature for 30 minutes before serving. Makes 1½ cups.

Serving Size: 1 teaspoon   **Calories:** 19   **Total Fat:** 1.8 grams (85%)
Sat. Fat: 1.1 grams   **Cholesterol:** 5.1 mgs.
Sodium: 52.7 mgs.   **Carbohydrates:** Less than 1 gram

Tarragon Butter

1 cup (2 sticks) Butter, at room temperature
2 teaspoons minced Shallots
2 teaspoons dried Tarragon Leaves

Combine all the ingredients in the work bowl of a food processor fitted with a steel blade. Process for 1 minute, scraping down the sides of the bowl as needed. Store in an air tight plastic container in the refrigerator. Let stand 30 minutes at room temperature before serving. Makes 1 cup.

Serving Size: 1 teaspoon   **Calories:** 34.1   **Total Fat:** 3.8 grams (99%)
Sat. Fat: 2.4 grams   **Cholesterol:** 10.4 mgs.
Sodium: 39.1 mgs.   **Carbohydrates:** Less than 1 gram

Preparation time: 10 minutes

Red Caviar Spread

8 ounces Cream Cheese, at room temperature
2 tablespoons Sour Cream
1 tablespoon Worcestershire Sauce
1 teaspoon minced Shallots
1 4-ounce jar Red Caviar

Combine the first four ingredients in the work bowl of a food processor fitted with a steel blade. Process for 1 minute, scraping down the sides of the bowl as needed. Put the mixture in a small bowl. Fold in the caviar with a rubber spatula. Store in an air tight plastic container in the refrigerator. Let stand 30 minutes at room temperature before serving. Makes 1¼ cups.

Serving Size: 1 teaspoon   **Calories:** 19.2   **Total Fat:** 1.8 grams (80%)
Sat. Fat: 1 gram   **Cholesterol:** 15.5 mgs.
Sodium: 42.5 mgs.   **Carbohydrates:** Less than 1 gram

Pesto Butter

¼ Cup Extra Virgin Olive Oil
3 teaspoons minced Garlic
2 tablespoons grated Parmesan Cheese
1 cup whole, fresh Basil Leaves (stems removed)
¼ cup fresh Parsley (stems removed)
1 tablespoon Pignoli (Pine Nuts)
½ teaspoon Coarse Salt
1 cup (2 sticks Butter), at room temperature

In the work bowl of a food processor fitted with a steel blade, combine all the ingredients except the butter, and pulse the machine for several seconds, until the mixture is coarsely chopped. Scrape down the sides of the work bowl, as needed. With the machine running, add the 2 sticks of butter, cut into large chunks. Process for 1 minute, or until well blended. Store in an air tight plastic container in the refrigerator. Let stand at room temperature for 30 minutes before serving. Makes about 1½ cups.

Serving Size: 1 teaspoon **Calories:** 31 **Total Fat:** 3.4 grams (97%)
Sat. Fat: 1.7 grams **Cholesterol:** 7.0 mgs.
Sodium: 44.3 mgs. **Carbohydrates:** Less than 1 gram

Preparation time: 10 minutes

Zingy Cheddar Butter

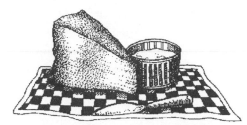

1 cup Butter, at room temperature
6 ounces shredded Extra Sharp Cheddar Cheese, at room temperature
2 teaspoons Horseradish

Combine all the ingredients in the work bowl of a food processor fitted with a steel blade. Process on medium speed for 60 seconds, scraping down the sides as needed. Store in an air-tight plastic container in the refrigerator. Let stand at room temperature for 30 minutes before serving.
Makes 1½ cups.

Serving Size: 1 tablespoon **Calories:** 96.4 **Total Fat:** 10 grams (92%)
Sat. Fat: 6.3 grams **Cholesterol:** 28.2 mgs.
Sodium: 123 mgs. **Carbohydrates:** Less than 1 gram

Tuna Butter

An old favorite!

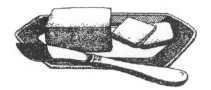

1 3¼-ounce can Tuna packed in Oil (do not drain)
¾ cup Butter (1½ sticks), at room temperature
1 rounded teaspoon Capers, drained and chopped

Place all the ingredients in the work bowl of a food processor fitted with a steel blade. Process for 60 seconds, or until smooth, scraping down the sides as needed. Store in an air-tight plastic container in the refrigerator. Makes about 1 ¼ cups.

Serving Size: 1 teaspoon   **Calories:** 24   **Total Fat:** 2.6 grams (93%)
Sat. Fat: 1.5 grams   **Cholesterol:** 7 mgs.
Sodium: 31.4 mgs.   **Carbohydrates:** Less than 1 gram

Lobster Butter

½ cup (1 stick) Butter, at room temperature
1 cup cooked and cleaned Lobster
(Shrimp or Crab may be substituted)
1 tablespoon fresh Lemon Juice
Dash of ground White Pepper
2 tablespoons chopped fresh Parsley

Combine all the ingredients in the work bowl of a food processor fitted with a steel blade. Pulse three or four times to begin mixing. Then scrape down the sides of the work bowl, and process for 1 minute, or until well combined. Store in an air tight plastic container in the refrigerator. Let stand at room temperature for 30 minutes before serving. Makes 1½ cups.

Serving Size: 1 teaspoon **Calories:** 37 **Total Fat:** 3.6 grams (80%)
Sat. Fat: 2.2 grams **Cholesterol:** 13.6 mgs.
Sodium: 57.4 mgs. **Carbohydrates:** Less than 1 gram

Index

Index

Q,R

S

U,V

W

X,Y,Z